ReactJS by Example - Building Modern Web Applications with React

Get up and running with ReactJS by developing five cutting-edge and responsive projects

Vipul A M

Prathamesh Sonpatki

BIRMINGHAM - MUMBAI

ReactJS by Example - Building Modern Web Applications with React

First published: April 2016

Production reference: 1110416

Published by Packt Publishing Ltd.
Livery Place
35 Livery Street
Birmingham B3 2PB, UK.

ISBN 978-1-78528-964-4

www.packtpub.com

Credits

Authors
Vipul A M
Prathamesh Sonpatki

Reviewers
Muhammad Arslan
Pawel Czekaj
Matt Goldspink

Commissioning Editor
Dipika Gaonkar

Acquisition Editor
Larissa Pinto

Content Development Editor
Mamata Walkar

Technical Editor
Bharat Patil

Copy Editor
Vibha Shukla

Project Coordinator
Kinjal Bari

Proofreader
Safis Editing

Indexer
Monica Ajmera Mehta

Graphics
Disha Haria

Production Coordinator
Arvindkumar Gupta

Cover Work
Arvindkumar Gupta

About the Authors

Vipul A M is Director at BigBinary. He is part of Rails Issues Team, and helps triaging issues. His spare time is spent exploring and contributing to many Open Source ruby projects, when not dabbling with React JS.

Vipul loves Ruby's vibrant community and helps in building PuneRb, is the founder of and runs RubyIndia Community Newsletter and RubyIndia Podcast, and organizes Deccan Ruby Conference in Pune.

He can be found @vipulnsward on twitter and on his site http://vipulnsward.com.

Prathamesh Sonpatki is Director at BigBinary. He builds web applications using Ruby on Rails and ReactJS. He loves learning new programming languages and contributing to open source.

He can be found @_cha1tanya on twitter.

About the Reviewers

Muhammad Arslan has been working in different roles: Senior IT-Developer, IT-Consultant, TechLead and Architect. He has vast experience of frontend and backend technologies and agile development. He has two master's degrees in Software Engineering and E-commerce. He has done his master's thesis in Usability and User Experience. He is also Oracle Certified Professional, Java Programmer (OCPJP).

He is currently working in biggest Nordic bank Nordea as Senior IT-Developer. He has previously worked in Digital River World Payments on bank gateway/iso connections and designed user interfaces. He worked in Accedo on SmartTV applications and application management products as well.

You can follow him on Twitter `@arslan_mecom` or you can check out his blog `http://www.jhear.com/`.

I would like to thank my mother, father (late), and my better half, for their continuous support for making me successful in my career.

Pawel Czekaj has a bachelor's degree in computer science. He is a web developer with strong backend (PHP, Java, MySQL, and Unix system) and frontend (AngularJS, Backbone, React.js, and jQuery) experience. He loves JavaScript, React.js, and Angular.js. Previously, he worked as a senior full stack web developer. Currently, he is working as a frontend developer for Cognifide and Toptal. You can contact him at `http://yadue.eu`.

Matt Goldspink is currently the lead engineer at Vlocity, Inc., based in San Francisco, working on their mobile and web platforms. Prior to this, he has held various roles at startups, banks, and also spent time as a technology trainer. Matt was the lead developer and architect for the award-winning mobile web platform for one of the world's leading investment banks.

www.PacktPub.com

Support files, eBooks, discount offers, and more

For support files and downloads related to your book, please visit www.PacktPub.com.

Did you know that Packt offers eBook versions of every book published, with PDF and ePub files available? You can upgrade to the eBook version at www.PacktPub.com and as a print book customer, you are entitled to a discount on the eBook copy. Get in touch with us at service@packtpub.com for more details.

At www.PacktPub.com, you can also read a collection of free technical articles, sign up for a range of free newsletters and receive exclusive discounts and offers on Packt books and eBooks.

https://www2.packtpub.com/books/subscription/packtlib

Do you need instant solutions to your IT questions? PacktLib is Packt's online digital book library. Here, you can search, access, and read Packt's entire library of books.

Why subscribe?

- Fully searchable across every book published by Packt
- Copy and paste, print, and bookmark content
- On demand and accessible via a web browser

Free access for Packt account holders

If you have an account with Packt at www.PacktPub.com, you can use this to access PacktLib today and view 9 entirely free books. Simply use your login credentials for immediate access.

Table of Contents

Preface

ReactJS is an open source JavaScript library that intends to bring aspects of reactive programming to web applications and sites. It aims to address the challenges encountered in developing single-page applications. React's core principles are declarative code, efficiency, flexibility, and improved developer experience.

What better way of learning a new technology than diving deep into it while working on something? This book will guide you with the help of different projects, each focusing on the specific features of React in your journey of mastering React. We will cover everything from JSX, add-ons, performance, and Redux.

Let the journey commence!

What this book covers

Chapter 1, *Getting Started with React*, covers the basics of ReactJS by building a simple app with static data. We will study top-level API of React and its basic building blocks.

Chapter 2, *JSX in Depth*, does a deep dive into JSX and how to use it with React. We will also look at a few gotchas that need to be considered while working with JSX.

Chapter 3, *Data Flow and Life Cycle Events*, focuses on data flow between React components and complete life cycle of a component.

Chapter 4, *Composite Dynamic Components and Forms*, shows how to build composite dynamic components using React with more focus on forms while building a form wizard application.

Chapter 5, *Mixins and the DOM*, covers mixins, refs, and how React interacts with DOM.

Chapter 6, React on the Server, uses React on the server side to render HTML and learn more about what server-side rendering brings to the table by building a search application based on Open Library Books API.

Chapter 7, React Addons, continues to use the search application and enhances it with various add-ons provided with React. We will study the use cases of these add-ons.

Chapter 8, Performance of React Apps, discusses everything about the performance of the React app by going deep into how React renders the content and helps in making our apps faster.

Chapter 9, React Router and Data Models, helps in building a Pinterest-style application and discusses routing using react-router. We will also discuss how various data models can be used with React, including Backbone models.

Chapter 10, Animation, focuses on making our Pinterest app more interactive with animations and how to use them effectively with React.

Chapter 11, React Tools, takes a step back and discusses various tools that we will use in our journey while working with React. We will study the tools such as Babel, ESLint, React dev tools, and Webpack.

Chapter 12, Flux, explains how to build a social media-tracker application while using the Flux architecture. We will discuss the need for the Flux architecture and what it brings to the table.

Chapter 13, Redux and React, covers using Redux — a popular state management library — to enhance the social media-tracker application further in order to use Redux-based state management.

What you need for this book

You will need to have a modern web browser, such as Chrome or Firefox, to run the examples from the book. You will also need to have Node.js — https://nodejs.org/en/ — installed with the npm package manager set up. Additional setup instructions can be found at https://github.com/bigbinary/reactjs-by-example.

Who this book is for

If you are a web developer and wish to learn ReactJS from scratch, then this book is tailor-made for you. Good understanding of JavaScript, HTML, and CSS is expected.

Conventions

In this book, you will find a number of text styles that distinguish between different kinds of information. Here are some examples of these styles and an explanation of their meaning.

Code words in text, database table names, folder names, filenames, file extensions, pathnames, dummy URLs, user input, and Twitter handles are shown as follows: "Notice, how we are using `this.props.headings` to access the passed information about headings."

A block of code is set as follows:

```
return <div>
        <h1>Recent Changes</h1>
          <table>
          ....
        </table>
        </div>
    ...
```

When we wish to draw your attention to a particular part of a code block, the relevant lines or items are set in bold:

```
TestUtils.Simulate.click(submitButton);
expect(app.state.searching).toEqual(true);
expect(app.state.searchCompleted).toEqual(false);
let spinner = TestUtils.findRenderedComponentWithType(app,
Spinner);
expect(spinner).toBeTruthy();
```

Any command-line input or output is written as follows:

```
Listening at localhost:9000
Hash: 8ec0d12965567260413b
Version: webpack 1.9.11
Time: 1639ms
```

New terms and **important words** are shown in bold. Words that you see on the screen, for example, in menus or dialog boxes, appear in the text like this: "Did you notice the **Auto-run JS** option?"

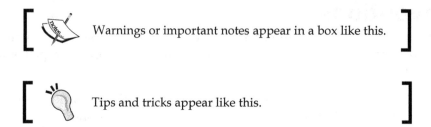

[Warnings or important notes appear in a box like this.]

[Tips and tricks appear like this.]

Reader feedback

Feedback from our readers is always welcome. Let us know what you think about this book—what you liked or disliked. Reader feedback is important for us as it helps us develop titles that you will really get the most out of.

To send us general feedback, simply e-mail feedback@packtpub.com, and mention the book's title in the subject of your message.

If there is a topic that you have expertise in and you are interested in either writing or contributing to a book, see our author guide at www.packtpub.com/authors.

Customer support

Now that you are the proud owner of a Packt book, we have a number of things to help you to get the most from your purchase.

Downloading the example code

You can download the example code files for this book from your account at http://www.packtpub.com. If you purchased this book elsewhere, you can visit http://www.packtpub.com/support and register to have the files e-mailed directly to you.

You can download the code files by following these steps:

1. Log in or register to our website using your e-mail address and password.
2. Hover the mouse pointer on the **SUPPORT** tab at the top.
3. Click on **Code Downloads & Errata**.
4. Enter the name of the book in the **Search** box.
5. Select the book for which you're looking to download the code files.
6. Choose from the drop-down menu where you purchased this book from.
7. Click on **Code Download**.

Once the file is downloaded, please make sure that you unzip or extract the folder using the latest version of:

- WinRAR / 7-Zip for Windows
- Zipeg / iZip / UnRarX for Mac
- 7-Zip / PeaZip for Linux

Errata

Although we have taken every care to ensure the accuracy of our content, mistakes do happen. If you find a mistake in one of our books—maybe a mistake in the text or the code—we would be grateful if you could report this to us. By doing so, you can save other readers from frustration and help us improve subsequent versions of this book. If you find any errata, please report them by visiting http://www.packtpub.com/submit-errata, selecting your book, clicking on the **Errata Submission Form** link, and entering the details of your errata. Once your errata are verified, your submission will be accepted and the errata will be uploaded to our website or added to any list of existing errata under the Errata section of that title.

To view the previously submitted errata, go to https://www.packtpub.com/books/content/support and enter the name of the book in the search field. The required information will appear under the **Errata** section.

Piracy

Piracy of copyrighted material on the Internet is an ongoing problem across all media. At Packt, we take the protection of our copyright and licenses very seriously. If you come across any illegal copies of our works in any form on the Internet, please provide us with the location address or website name immediately so that we can pursue a remedy.

Please contact us at copyright@packtpub.com with a link to the suspected pirated material.

We appreciate your help in protecting our authors and our ability to bring you valuable content.

Questions

If you have a problem with any aspect of this book, you can contact us at questions@packtpub.com, and we will do our best to address the problem.

1
Getting Started with React

Web development has seen a huge advent of **Single Page Application** (**SPA**) in the past couple of years. Early development was simple — reload a complete page to perform a change in the display or perform a user action. The problem with this was a huge round-trip time for the complete request to reach the web server and back to the client.

Then came AJAX, which sent a request to the server, and could update parts of the page without reloading the current page. Moving in the same direction, we saw the emergence of the SPAs.

Wrapping up the heavy frontend content and delivering it to the client browser just once, while maintaining a small channel for communication with the server based on any event; this is usually complemented by thin API on the web server.

The growth in such apps has been complemented by JavaScript libraries and frameworks such as Ext JS, KnockoutJS, BackboneJS, AngularJS, EmberJS, and more recently, React and Polymer.

Let's take a look at how React fits in this ecosystem and get introduced to it in this chapter.

In this chapter, we will cover the following topics:

- What is React and why do we use React?
- Data flows in the component
- Component displays the view based on state of the component
- Component defines display of the view, irrespective of data contained, thus reducing the dependency and complexity of state for display
- User interactions may change state of component from handlers
- Components are reused and re-rendered

What is React?

ReactJS tries to solve the problem from the *View* layer. It can very well be defined and used as the *V* in any of the *MVC* frameworks. It's not opinionated about how it should be used. It creates abstract representations of views. It breaks down parts of the view in the *Components*. These components encompass both the logic to handle the display of view and the view itself. It can contain data that it uses to render the state of the app.

To avoid complexity of interactions and subsequent render processing required, React does a full render of the application. It maintains a simple flow of work.

React is founded on the idea that DOM manipulation is an expensive operation and should be minimized. It also recognizes that optimizing DOM manipulation by hand will result in a lot of *boilerplate* code, which is error-prone, boring, and repetitive.

React solves this by giving the developer a virtual DOM to render to instead of the actual DOM. It finds difference between the real DOM and virtual DOM and conducts the minimum number of DOM operations required to achieve the new state.

React is also declarative. When the data changes, React conceptually hits the refresh button and knows to only update the changed parts.

This simple flow of data, coupled with dead simple display logic, makes development with ReactJS straightforward and simple to understand.

Who uses React? If you've used any of the services such as Facebook, Instagram, Netflix, Alibaba, Yahoo, E-Bay, Khan-Academy, AirBnB, Sony, and Atlassian, you've already come across and used React on the Web.

In just under a year, React has seen adoption from major Internet companies in their core products.

In its first-ever conference, React also announced the development of React Native. React Native allows the development of mobile applications using React. It transpiles React code to the native application code, such as Objective-C for iOS applications.

At the time of writing this, Facebook already uses React Native in its Groups and Ads Manager app.

In this book, we will be following a conversation between two developers, Mike and Shawn. Mike is a senior developer at Adequate Consulting and Shawn has just joined the company. Mike will be mentoring Shawn and conducting pair programming with him.

When Shawn meets Mike and ReactJS

It's a bright day at Adequate Consulting. Its' also Shawn's first day at the company. Shawn had joined Adequate to work on its amazing products and also because it uses and develops exciting new technologies.

After onboarding the company, Shelly, the CTO, introduced Shawn to Mike. Mike, a senior developer at Adequate, is a jolly man, who loves exploring new things.

"So Shawn, here's Mike", said Shelly. "He'll be mentoring you as well as pairing with you on development. We follow pair programming, so expect a lot of it with him. He's an excellent help."

With that, Shelly took leave.

"Hey Shawn!" Mike began, "are you all set to begin?"

"Yeah, all set! So what are we working on?"

"Well we are about to start working on an app using `https://openlibrary.org/`. Open Library is collection of the world's classic literature. It's an open, editable library catalog for all the books. It's an initiative under `https://archive.org/` and lists free book titles. We need to build an app to display the most recent changes in the record by Open Library. You can call this the **Activities** page. Many people contribute to Open Library. We want to display the changes made by these users to the books, addition of new books, edits, and so on, as shown in the following screenshot:

Recent Changes
Author Merges | Books Added | Covers Added | Lists

By Humans   BY BOTS   EVERYTHING

WHEN	WHAT	WHO	¿QUÉ?
6 seconds ago	/people/sunshine0427	Sun-Hei Bamfo	Created new account.
10 seconds ago	To Read (list) – diff	Paul W. Jeffries	Added Tennis, anyone? to the list.
20 seconds ago	To Read (list) – diff	Paul W. Jeffries	Added The Chinook to the list.
32 seconds ago	/people/asharr	Al Sharr	Created new account.
35 seconds ago	To Read (list) – diff	Paul W. Jeffries	Added The Aztecs to the list.
2 minutes ago	The Shabbat primer – diff	Cheryl Conway	Added new cover
2 minutes ago	/people/umbravo	umbravo	Created new account.
3 minutes ago	A sermon being an incouragement for Protestants – expand	LeadSongDog	
4 minutes ago	The substance of a sermon, being an incouragement for Protestants – expand	LeadSongDog	
4 minutes ago	/people/jayrey55	Joshua Reynolds	Created new account.
4 minutes ago	The substance of a discourse being an incouragement for Protestants – expand	LeadSongDog	
5 minutes ago	/people/kaleem1	Kaleem Khodabux	Created new account.
5 minutes ago	/people/stephaniein29	Stephanie Jacobson	Created new account.
5 minutes ago	/people/ghal6	Gregor Halfmann	Created new account.

"Oh nice! What are we using to build it?"

"Open Library provides us with a neat REST API that we can consume to fetch the data. We are just going to build a simple page that displays the fetched data and format it for display. I've been experimenting and using ReactJS for this. Have you used it before?"

"Nope. However, I have heard about it. Isn't it the one from Facebook and Instagram?"

"That's right. It's an amazing way to define our UI. As the app isn't going to have much of logic on the server or perform any display, it is an easy option to use it."

"As you've not used it before, let me provide you a quick introduction."

"Have you tried services such as JSBin and JSFiddle before?"

"No, but I have seen them."

"Cool. We'll be using one of these, therefore, we don't need anything set up on our machines to start with."

"Let's try on your machine", Mike instructed. "Fire up `http://jsbin. com/?html,output`"

"You should see something similar to the tabs and panes to code on and their output in adjacent pane."

"Go ahead and make sure that the **HTML**, **JavaScript**, and **Output** tabs are clicked and you can see three frames for them so that we are able to edit HTML and JS and see the corresponding output."

"That's nice."

"Yeah, good thing about this is that you don't need to perform any setups. Did you notice the **Auto-run JS** option? Make sure its selected. This option causes JSBin to reload our code and see its output so that we don't need to keep saying **Run with JS** to execute and see its output."

"Ok."

Requiring React library

"Alright then! Let's begin. Go ahead and change the title of the page, to say, React JS Example. Next, we need to set up and we require the React library in our file."

"React's homepage is located at http://facebook.github.io/react/. Here, we'll also locate the downloads available for us so that we can include them in our project. There are different ways to include and use the library.

We can make use of bower or install via npm. We can also just include it as an individual download, directly available from the fb.me domain. There are development versions that are full version of the library as well as production version which is its minified version. There is also its version of add-on. We'll take a look at this later though."

"Let's start by using the development version, which is the unminified version of the React source. Add the following to the file header:"

```
<script src="http://fb.me/react-0.13.0.js"></script>
```

"Done".

"Awesome, let's see how this looks."

```
<!DOCTYPE html>
<html>
<head>
  <script src="http://fb.me/react-0.13.0.js"></script>
  <meta charset="utf-8">
  <title>React JS Example</title>
</head>
<body>

</body>
</html>
```

Building our first component

"So Shawn, we are all set to begin. Let's build our very first React App. Go ahead and add the following code to the JavaScript section of JSBin:"

```
var App = React.createClass({
  render: function(){
```

```
        return(React.createElement("div", null, "Welcome to Adequate,
    Mike!"));
    }
});
```

```
React.render(React.createElement(App), document.body);
```

"Here it is. You should see the output section of the page showing something similar to the following:"

```
    Welcome to Adequate, Mike!
```

"Nice Mike. I see that we are making use of this React object to create classes?"

"That's right. We are creating, what are called as Components in React."

"The entry point to the ReactJS library is the React object. Once the `react.js` library is included, it is made available to us in the global JavaScript namespace."

"`React.createClass` creates a component with the given specification. The component must implement the render method that returns a single child element as follows:"

```
var App = React.createClass({
   render: function(){
       return(React.createElement("div", null, "Welcome to Adequate,
   Mike!"));
   }
});
```

React will take care of calling the render method of the component to generate the HTML."

 Even if the render method needs to return a single child, that single child can have an arbitrarily deep structure to contain full-fledged HTML page parts.

"Here, we are making use of `React.createElement` to create our content. It's a singleton method that allows us to create a `div` element with the "`Welcome to Adequate, Mike!` contents. `React.createElement` creates a `ReactElement`, which is an internal representation of the DOM element used by React. We are passing null as the second argument. This is used to pass and specify attributes for the element. Right now, we are leaving it as blank to create a simple div."

"The type of `ReactElement` can be either a valid HTML tag name like span, div, h1 and so on or a component created by `React.createClass` itself."

"Once we are done creating the component, it can be displayed using the `React.render` method as follows:"

```
React.render(React.createElement(App), document.body);
```

"Here, a new `ReactElement` is created for the `App` component that we have created previously and it is then rendered into the HTML element—`document.body`. This is called the `mountNode`, or mount point for our component, and acts as the root node. Instead of passing `document.body` directly as a container for the component, any other DOM element can also be passed."

"Mike, go ahead and change the text passed to the div as `Hello React World!`. We should start seeing the change and it should look something similar to the following:"

```
Hello React World!
```

"Nice."

"Mike, while constructing the first component, we also got an overview of React's top-level API, that is, making use of `React.createClass`, `React.createElement`, and `React.render`."

"Now, the component that we just built to display this hello message is pretty simple and straightforward. However, the syntax can get challenging and it keeps growing when building complex things. Here's where JSX comes in handy."

"JSX?"

"JSX is an XML-like syntax extension to ECMAScript without any defined semantics. It has a concise and familiar syntax with plain HTML and it's familiar for designers or non-programmers. It can also be used directly from our JavaScript file!"

"What? Isn't it bad?"

"Well, time to rethink the best practices. That's right, we will be bringing our view and its HTML in the JavaScript file!"

"Let's see how to start using it. Go ahead and change the contents of our JavaScript file as follows:"

```
var App = React.createClass({
  render: function(){
    return <div>
     Hello, from Shawn!
    </div>;
  }
```

```
    });

    React.render(React.createElement(App), document.body);
```

"As you can see, what we did here was that instead of using `createElement`, we directly wrote the `div` tag. This is very similar to writing HTML markup directly. It also works right out of the JavaScript file."

"Mike, the code is throwing some errors on JSBin."

"Oh, right. We need to make use of the JSX transformer library so that React and the browser can understand the syntax. In our case, we need to change the type of JavaScript, which we are using, to be used to interpret this code. What we need to do is change from **JavaScript** to **JSX (React)**, from the dropdown on the JavaScript frame header, as follows:"

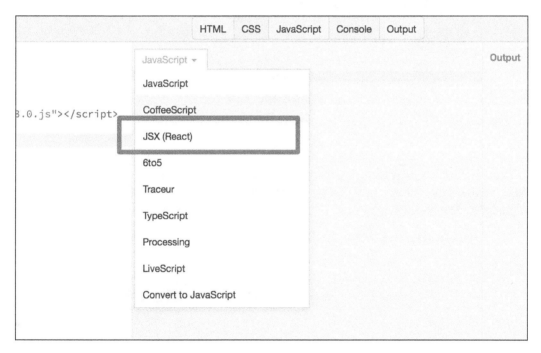

"That should do it."

"Looks good, Mike. It's working."

"Now you will see something similar to the following:"

```
    Hello, from Shawn!
```

Back to work

"That's good to start, Shawn. Let's move back to the task of building our app using Open Library's Recent changes API now. We already have a basic prototype ready without using ReactJS."

"We will be slowly replacing parts of it using ReactJS."

"This is how the information is displayed right now, using server-side logic, as follows:"

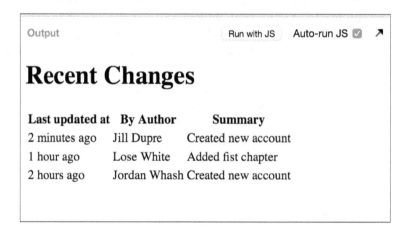

"First task that we have is to display the information retrieved from the Open Library Recent Changes API in a table using ReactJS similar to how it's displayed right now using server-side."

"We will be fetching the data from the Open Library API similar to the following:"

```
var data = [{ "when": "2 minutes ago",
           "who": "Jill Dupre",
           "description": "Created new account"
         },
         {
           "when": "1 hour ago",
           "who": "Lose White",
           "description": "Added fist chapter"
         },
         {
           "when": "2 hours ago",
           "who": "Jordan Whash",
           "description": "Created new account"
         }];
```

"Let's use this to prototype our app for now. Before that, let's take a look at the simple HTML version of this app. In our `React.render` method, we start returning a table element, as follows:"

```
var App = React.createClass({

  render: function(){
  return <table>
  <thead>
    <th>When</th>
    <th>Who</th>
    <th>Description</th>
  </thead>
    <tr>
      <td>2 minutes ago</td>
      <td>Jill Dupre</td>
      <td>Created new account</td>
    </tr>
    <tr>
      <td>1 hour ago</td>
      <td>Lose White</td>
      <td>Added fist chapter</td>
    </tr>
    <tr>
      <td>2 hours ago</td>
      <td>Jordan Whash</td>
      <td>Created new account</td>
    </tr>
  </table>
    }
});
```

"This should start displaying our table with three rows. Now, go ahead and add a heading at top of this table from the `React App`, as follows:"

```
...
return <h1>Recent Changes</h1>
            <table>
            ....
            </table>

...
```

"There, something like that?" asked Shawn. "Oh, that didn't work."

"That's because React expends our render method to always return a single HTML element. In this case, after you added the h1 heading, our app started returning two elements, which is wrong. There'll be many cases when you will come across this. To avoid this, just wrap the elements in a div or span tag. The main idea is that we just want to return a single element from the render method."

"Got it. Something like this?"

```
...
return <div>
          <h1>Recent Changes</h1>
            <table>
          ....
          </table>
          </div>
...
```

Displaying static data

"Awesome! Looks good. Now, let's change our table that is displaying static information, to start fetching and displaying this information in the rows from the JSON data that we had before."

"We'll define this data in the render method itself and see how we would be using it to create our table. We'll basically just be looping over the data and creating elements, that is, table rows in our case, for the individual data set of events. Something like this:"

```
...
var data = [{ "when": "2 minutes ago",
          "who": "Jill Dupre",
          "description": "Created new account"
        },
        {
          "when": "1 hour ago",
          "who": "Lose White",
          "description": "Added fist chapter"
        },
        {
          "when": "2 hours ago",
          "who": "Jordan Whash",
          "description": "Created new account"
        }];

var rows = data.map(function(row){
```

```
   return  <tr>
      <td>{row.when}</td>
      <td>{row.who}</td>
      <td>{row.description}</td>
    </tr>
   });
  ...
```

"Notice how we are using {} here. {} is used in JSX to embed dynamic information in our view template. We can use it to embed the JavaScript objects in our views, for example, the name of a person or heading of this table. As you can see, what we are doing here is using the map function to loop over the dataset that we have. Then, we are returning a table row, constructed from the information available from the row object – the details about when the event was created, who created it and event description."

"We are using JSX syntax here to construct the rows of table. However, it is not used as the final return value from render function."

"That's correct, Shawn. React with JSX allows us to arbitrarily create elements to be used in our views, in our case, creating it dynamically from the dataset that we have. The rows variable now contains a part of view that we had used at a different place. We can also build another component of the view on top of it."

"That's the beauty of it. React allows us to dynamically create, use, and reuse the parts of views. This is helpful to build our views, part by part, in a systematic way."

"Now, after we are done with building our rows, we can use them in our final render call."

"So now, the return statement will look something similar to the following:"

```
  ...
  return <table>
  <thead>
    <th>When</th>
    <th>Who</th>
    <th>Description</th>
  </thead>
{rows}
  </table>
  ...
```

"Here's how the complete render method now looks after building up rows with static data:"

```
render: function(){
var data = [{ "when": "2 minutes ago",
             "who": "Jill Dupre",
             "description": "Created new account"
           },
           {
             "when": "1 hour ago",
             "who": "Lose White",
             "description": "Added fist chapter"
           },
           {
             "when": "2 hours ago",
             "who": "Jordan Whash",
             "description": "Created new account"
           }];

var rows = data.map(function(row){
return   <tr>
    <td>{row.when}</td>
    <td>{row.who}</td>
    <td>{row.description}</td>
  </tr>
  })
return <table>
<thead>
  <th>When</th>
  <th>Who</th>
  <th>Description</th>
</thead>
{rows}
</table>}
```

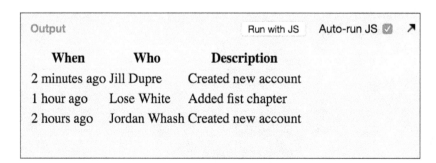

"That's starting to look like where we want to reach."

Passing data to components

"Do we define our data and everything else in the render method?"

"I was just getting to that. Our component should not contain this information. The information should be passed as a parameter to it."

"React allows us to pass the JavaScript objects to components. These objects would be passed when we call the `React.render` method and create an instance of the `<App>` component. The following is how we can pass objects to it:"

```
React.render(<App title='Recent  Changes'/>, document.body);
```

"Notice how are using the `<App/>` syntax here, instead of `createElement`. As I mentioned previously, we can create elements from our components and represent them using JSX as done earlier."

```
React.render(React.createElement(App), document.body)
```

"The preceding code becomes the following:"

```
React.render(<App/>, document.body)
```

"That looks even more cleaner", said Shawn.

"As you can see, we are passing the title for our table as the `title` parameter, followed by the contents of the title. React makes this data passed to the component as something called `props`. The `props`, short for properties, are a component's configuration options that are passed to the component when initializing it."

"These `props` are just plain JavaScript objects. They are made accessible to us within our component via the `this.props` method. Let's try accessing this from the `render` method, as follows:"

```
...
  render: function(){
   console.log(this.props.title);
  }
...
```

"That should start logging the title that we passed to the component to the console."

"Now, let's try to abstract the headings as well as the JSON data out of the `render` method and start passing them to the component, as follows:"

```
var data = [{ "when": "2 minutes ago",
              "who": "Jill Dupre",
              "description": "Created new account"
            },
            ....
          }];
var headings = ['When', 'Who', 'Description']
<App headings = {headings} data = {data} />
```

"There. We pulled the data out of the `render` method and are now passing it to our component."

"We defined the dynamic headers for our table that we will start using in the component."

"Here the curly braces, used to pass the parameters to our component, are used to specify the JavaScript expressions that will be evaluated and then used as attribute values."

"For example, the preceding JSX code will get translated into JavaScript by React, as follows:"

```
React.createElement(App, { headings: headings, data: data });
```

"We will revisit props later. However, right now, let's move on to complete our component."

"Now, using the passed data and headings via props, we need to generate the table structure in the app's `render` method."

"Let's generate the headings first, as follows:"

```
var App = React.createClass({

  render: function(){
    var headings = this.props.headings.map(function(heading) {
      return (<th>
              {heading}
              </th>);
    });
  }
});
```

"Notice, how we are using `this.props.headings` to access the passed information about headings. Now let's create rows of the table similar to what we were doing earlier:"

```
var App = React.createClass({

  render: function(){
      var headings = this.props.headings.map(function(heading) {
          return(<th>
                  {heading}
                  </th>);
      });

      var rows = this.props.data.map(function(change) {
          return(<tr>
                  <td> { change.when } </td>
                  <td> { change.who } </td>
                  <td> { change.description } </td>
                  </tr>);
      });
  }
});
```

"Finally, let's put the headings and rows together in our table."

```
var App = React.createClass({

  render: function(){
      var headings = this.props.headings.map(function(heading) {
          return(<th>
                  {heading}
                  </th>);
      });

      var rows = this.props.data.map(function(change) {
          return(<tr>
                  <td> {change.when} </td>
                  <td> {change.who} </td>
                  <td> {change.description} </td>
                  </tr>);
      });

      return(<table>
              {headings}
```

```
            {rows}
          </table>);

    }
});
```

```
React.render(<App headings = {headings} data = {data} />,
                document.body);
```

"The table is now displayed with the passed dynamic headers and JSON data."

"The headings can be changed to `["Last change at", "By Author", "Summary"]` and the table in our view will get updated automatically."

"Alright, Shawn, go ahead and add a title to our table. Make sure to pass it from the props."

"Ok," said Shawn.

"Now, the render method will be changed to the following:"

```
  ...
  return <div>
              <h1>
                {this.props.title}
              </h1>
              <table>
                <thead>
                  {headings}
                </thead>
                {rows}
              </table>
          </div>
  ...
```

"While the call to `React.render` will change to the following:"

```
var title =   'Recent Changes';
React.render(<App headings={headings} data={data} title={title}/>,
document.body);
```

"Awesome. You are starting to get a hang of it. Let's see how this looks in completion shall we?"

```
var App = React.createClass({
  render: function(){
      var headings = this.props.headings.map(function(heading)  {
```

```
            return(<th>
                    {heading}
                    </th>);
        });

    var rows = this.props.data.map(function(row){
    return  <tr>
        <td>{row.when}</td>
        <td>{row.who}</td>
        <td>{row.description}</td>
      </tr>

    })
 return <div><h1>{this.props.title}</h1><table>
 <thead>
{headings}
 </thead>
{rows}
 </table></div>
    }
});
    var data = [{ "when": "2 minutes ago",
                "who": "Jill Dupre",
                "description": "Created new account"
            },
            {
                "when": "1 hour ago",
                "who": "Lose White",
                "description": "Added fist chapter"
            },
            {
                "when": "2 hours ago",
                "who": "Jordan Whash",
                "description": "Created new account"
            }];

var headings = ["Last updated at", "By Author", "Summary"]
var title = "Recent Changes";
React.render(<App headings={headings} data={data} title={title}/>,
document.body);
```

"We should again start seeing something as follows:"

"Here we have it, Shawn. Our very first component using React!", said Mike.

"This looks amazing. I can't wait to try out more things in React!", exclaimed Shawn.

Summary

In this chapter, we started with React and built our first component. In the process, we studied the top-level API of React to construct components and elements. We used JSX to construct the components. We saw how to display static information using React and then gradually replaced all the static information with dynamic information using props. In the end, we were able to tie all ends together and display mock data in the format that is returned from Open Library's Recent Changes API using React.

In the next chapter, we will dive deep into JSX internals and continue building our application for Recent Changes API.

2
JSX in Depth

In the first chapter, we built our first component using React. We saw how using JSX makes the development easy. In this chapter, we will dive deep into JSX.

JavaScript XML (JSX) is an XML syntax that constructs the markup in React components. React works without JSX, but using JSX makes it easy to read and write the React components as well as structure them just like any other HTML element.

In this chapter, we will cover following points:

- Why JSX?
- Transforming JSX into JavaScript
- Specifying HTML tags and React components
- Multiple components
- Different types of JSX tags
- Using JavaScript expressions inside JSX
- Namespaced components
- Spread attributes
- CSS styles and JSX
- JSX Gotchas

At the end of the chapter, we will get familiar with the JSX syntax, how it should be used with React, and best practices of using it. We will also study some of the corner cases that one can run into while using JSX.

Why JSX?

Shawn had a great first day and he was just getting started with the next one at Adequate Consulting. With a mug of coffee, he startled Mike.

"Hey Mike, I saw that we used JSX for building our first component. Why should we use JSX when React has `React.createElement`?"

"You can use React without using JSX. But JSX makes it easy to build React components. It reduces the amount of code required to write. It looks like HTML markup. Its syntax is simple and concise and it's very easy to visualize the components that are getting built."

"Take an example of the render function of a component without using JSX."

```
// render without JSX
render: function(){
    return(React.createElement("div",
                               null,
                               "Hello React World!"));
}
```

"With JSX, it looks much better."

```
// render with JSX
render: function(){
    return <div>
      Hello React World
    </div>;
  }
```

"Compared to the previous non-JSX example, the JSX code is much more readable, easy to understand, and close to the actual HTML markup."

"The similarity between JSX and HTML markup means that non-developers such as UI and UX designers in the team can contribute to a project using JSX. Having XML-like tag syntax also makes reading large component trees easier compared to the function calls or object literals in JavaScript." explained Mike.

"Yeah. The syntax does look familiar. We will be using JSX all the way in our projects right?"

"Yes, we will", remarked Mike.

Transforming JSX into JavaScript

"Shawn, as I mentioned, the JSX is transformed to the native JavaScript syntax."

```
// Input (JSX):
var app = <App name="Mike" />;
```

"This will eventually get transformed to"

```
// Output (JS):
var app = React.createElement(App, {name:"Mike"});
```

Downloading the example code

You can download the example code files for this book from your account at http://www.packtpub.com. If you purchased this book elsewhere, you can visit http://www.packtpub.com/support and register to have the files e-mailed directly to you.

You can download the code files by following these steps:

- Log in or register to our website using your e-mail address and password.
- Hover the mouse pointer on the **SUPPORT** tab at the top.
- Click on **Code Downloads & Errata**.
- Enter the name of the book in the **Search** box.
- Select the book for which you're looking to download the code files.
- Choose from the drop-down menu where you purchased this book from.
- Click on **Code Download**.

Once the file is downloaded, please make sure that you unzip or extract the folder using the latest version of:

- WinRAR / 7-Zip for Windows
- Zipeg / iZip / UnRarX for Mac
- 7-Zip / PeaZip for Linux

"If you would like to see this live in action, try this example at https://babeljs.io/repl/. It's a live REPL that can transform a JSX code to the native JavaScript code."

"There is another editor available for converting HTML to JSX. You can check it out at `http://facebook.github.io/react/html-jsx.html`. This allows you to paste an arbitrary HTML code that gets converted to JSX with extraction of styles, classes, and other information and then create a component on top of it." said Mike.

"Pretty handy. However, this is just for ease of development, right? What happens when we deploy our code?" asked Shawn.

"JSX is not meant to be compiled at runtime. Though there is a JSX transformer that converts JSX to JavaScript in a browser. Using it to compile JSX at runtime in the browser would slow down our application. We will use tools such as Babel, which is a JavaScript transpiler to convert our JSX code to the native JavaScript code before deploying the application."

HTML tags vs React components

"Mike, I am intrigued by one more thing. In JSX, we are mixing the React components as if they are simple HTML tags. We did this in our first component."

```
ReactDOM.render(<App headings = {['When', 'Who', 'Description']}
                    data = {data} />,
            document.getElementById('container'));
```

"The `App` tag is not a valid HTML tag here. But this still works."

"Yes. That's because we can specify both HTML tags and React components in JSX. There is a subtle difference though. HTML tags start with a lowercase letter and React components start with an uppercase letter." Mike explained.

```
// Specifying HTML tags
render: function(){
    return(<table className = 'table'>
        .....
        </table>);
}

// Specifying React components
var App = React.createClass({..});
ReactDOM.render(<App headings = {['When', 'Who', 'Description']}
                    data = {data} />,
                document.getElementById('container'));
```

"That's the primary difference. JSX uses this convention to differentiate between the local component classes and HTML tags."

Self closing tag

"Another thing that you must have noticed is how the component tag is closed in `ReactDOM.render`" added Mike.

```
ReactDOM.render(<App .../>, document.getElementById('container'));
```

"As JSX is based on XML, it allows adding a self-closing tag. All the component tags must be closed either with self-closing format or with a closing tag."

"Thanks Mike! Things make much more sense now."

Multiple components

"Shawn, let's get back to our application. We are using almost the same code from last time but you can set up a new JSBin. We have included the latest React library and bootstrap library in the HTML tab. We have also added a container element, which we will render our React app."

```html
<!DOCTYPE html>
<html>
  <head>
    <script src="https://code.jquery.com/jquery.min.js"></script>
    <link href="https://netdna.bootstrapcdn.com/twitter-
bootstrap/2.3.2/css/bootstrap-combined.min.css" rel="stylesheet"
type="text/css" />
    <script src="https://netdna.bootstrapcdn.com/twitter-
bootstrap/2.3.2/js/bootstrap.min.js"></script>
    <script src="//fb.me/react-with-addons-0.14.3.js"></script>
    <script src="//fb.me/react-dom-0.14.3.js"></script>
    <meta charset="utf-8">
    <meta name="viewport" content="width=device-width">
    <title>JSX in Detail</title>
  </head>
  <body>
    <div id="container">
    </div>
  </body>
</html>
```

"Right now, we are only using a single component to display the data from the recent changes API."

```js
var App = React.createClass({
  render: function(){
    var headings = this.props.headings.map(function(heading) {
```

```
        return(<th>
          {heading}
        </th>);
    });

    var rows = this.props.data.map(function(row){
        return   <tr>
          <td>{row.when}</td>
          <td>{row.who}</td>
          <td>{row.description}</td>
        </tr>

    })
        return <div><h1>{this.props.title}</h1><table>
          <thead>
            {headings}
          </thead>
          {rows}
        </table></div>
    }
});
```

"Let's split this single component into small composable components. These simple modular components will use other modular components with well-defined self-contained interfaces."

"Got it" said Shawn.

"Ok. The first step is trying to identify the different components that are present in our single component."

"Currently, our render method lists `tableHeadings` and `tableRows` as the children of table element."

```
    return(<table>
              {tableHeadings}
              {tableRows}
          </table>);
```

"I guess we will make the components for the headings and rows?" Shawn asked.

"Yes. But we can go one step further. Both headings and rows are lists of still smaller units, a `Heading` and a `Row` tag, respectively. It can be visualized as follows:"

```
<table>
  <Headings>
    <Heading/>
    <Heading/>
  </Headings>
  <Rows >
    <Row/>
    <Row/>
  </Rows>
</table>
```

"Makes sense, Mike. Let me try to create `Heading` now."

"Sure, go ahead."

```
var Heading = React.createClass({
  render: function() {
    return(<th>{heading}</th>);
  }
});
```

"Mike, I think this will work, except the heading. I am not sure how to render the actual heading in the `<th>` tag."

"Don't worry about it. Let's just assume that it will be passed as props to the `Heading` component."

"Sure. Here is the `Heading` component then:"

```
var Heading = React.createClass({
  render: function() {
    return(<th>{this.props.heading}</th>);
  }
});
```

"Perfect! The `Row` component will also be similar to `Heading`. It will get the `changeSet` object in its props"

```
var Row = React.createClass({
  render: function() {
    return(<tr>
            <td>{this.props.changeSet.when}</td>
            <td>{this.props.changeSet.who}</td>
```

```
            <td>{this.props.changeSet.description}</td>
        </tr>);
    }
});
```

"Shawn, we are done with lowest-level components. Now, it's time to move up a level. Let's build `Headings` first."

"Similar to how a `Heading` component will get its title in props, `Headings` will get a list of titles passed to it."

```
var Headings = React.createClass({
  render: function() {
    var headings = this.props.headings.map(function(heading) {
      return(<Heading heading = {heading}/>);
    });

    return (<thead><tr>{headings}</tr><thead>);
  }
});
```

"We are iterating over the list of titles and converting them into a list of the `Heading` components. The `Headings` component is controlling how the props are passed to the individual `Heading` components. In a sense, individual `Heading` components are owned by `Headings`." explained Mike.

"In React, an owner is the component that sets props of other components. We can also say that if the X component is present in the `render()` method of the Y component, then Y owns X." Mike further added.

"Shawn, go ahead and build the Rows component similar to `Headings`."

"Here you go:"

```
var Rows = React.createClass({
  render: function() {
    var rows = this.props.changeSets.map(function(changeSet) {
      return(<Row changeSet = {changeSet}/>);
    });
    return ({rows});
  }
});
```

"There is just one issue. You can't render the rows as it's a collection of components. Remember that the `render()` function can only render one tag" Mike said.

"I guess I should wrap the rows in a `<tbody>` tag.", Shawn."

```
var Rows = React.createClass({
  render: function() {
    var rows = this.props.changeSets.map(function(changeSet) {
      return (<Row changeSet = {changeSet}/>);
    });

    return (<tobdy>{rows}</tbody>);
  }
});
```

"Perfect. We have almost everything now. Let's finish it by adding the top-level `App` component."

```
var App = React.createClass({
  render: function(){
    return <table className = 'table'>
             <Headings headings = {this.props.headings} />
             <Rows changeSets = {this.props.changeSets} />
           </table>;
  }
});
```

"Here's how our complete code looks now:"

```
var Heading = React.createClass({
  render: function() {
    return <th>{this.props.heading}</th>;
  }
});

var Headings = React.createClass({
  render: function() {
    var headings = this.props.headings.map(function(name) {
      return <Heading heading = {name}/>;
    });
    return <thead><tr>{headings}</tr></thead>;
  }
});

var Row = React.createClass({
  render: function() {
    return <tr>
             <td>{this.props.changeSet.when}</td>
```

```
            <td>{this.props.changeSet.who}</td>
            <td>{this.props.changeSet.description}</td>
          </tr>;
      }
  });

  var Rows = React.createClass({
    render: function() {
      var rows = this.props.changeSets.map(function(changeSet) {
        return(<Row changeSet = {changeSet}/>);
      });
      return <tbody>{rows}</tbody>;
    }
  });


  var App = React.createClass({
    render: function() {
      return <table className = 'table'>
              <Headings headings = {this.props.headings} />
              <Rows changeSets = {this.props.changeSets} />
            </table>;
      }
  });

  var data = [{ "when": "2 minutes ago",
                "who": "Jill Dupre",
                "description": "Created new account"
              },
              {
                "when": "1 hour ago",
                "who": "Lose White",
                "description": "Added fist chapter"
            }];
  var headings = ['When', 'Who', 'Description'];

  ReactDOM.render(<App headings = {headings}
                       changeSets = {data} />,
                                        document.
  getElementById('container'));
```

"Shawn, I think you have understood the power of composability of components now. It makes our UI easy to reason with and easy to reuse and compose. We will be using this philosophy throughout with React."

"I agree. Every component does one thing right and in the end, all of them get composed together so that the whole application is built. Different parts of the code get separated in such a way that they don't interfere with each other."

JavaScript expressions

"Shawn, let's discuss a bit about how we have rendered the Rows and Headings tag."

```
render: function() {
    var headings = this.props.headings.map(function(name) {
      return(<Heading heading = {name}/>);
    });

  return <tr>{headings}</tr>;
  }
```

"We are rendering {headings}, which is a list of React components, directly by adding them in curly braces as children of the <tr> tag. These expressions that are used to specify the child components are called child expressions."

"There is another category of expressions called as JavaScript expressions. These are simple expressions used for passing props or evaluating some JavaScript code that can be used as an attribute value."

```
// Passing props as expressions
ReactDOM.render(<App headings = {['When', 'Who', 'Description']}
               data = {data} />,
               document.getElementById('container'));


// Evaluating expressions
ReactDOM.render(<App headings = {['When', 'Who', 'Description']}
               data = {data.length > 0 ? data : ''} />,
               document.getElementById('container'));
```

"Anything that is present in curly braces is evaluated by JSX. It works for both children expressions as well as JavaScript expressions," added Mike.

"Thanks for the detailed explanation. I have a query though. Is there any way to write comments in the JSX code? I mean, we may not need it all the time, but knowing how to add comments might be handy," Shawn asked.

"Remember the curly braces rule. Comments are simply just JavaScript expressions. When we are in a child element, just wrap the comments in the curly braces."

```
render: function() {
    return(<th>
            {/* This is a comment */}
            {this.props.heading}
        </th>);
}
```

"You can also add comments in a JSX tag. There is no need to wrap them in curly braces in this case," Mike added.

```
ReactDOM.render(<App
                /* Multi
                    Line
                    Comment
                */
                headings = {headings}
                changeSets = {data} />,
            document.getElementById('container'));
```

Namespaced components

"Shawn, you must have used modules and packages in languages such as Ruby and Java. The idea behind these concepts is to create a namespace hierarchy of code such that the code from one module or package doesn't interfere with another."

"Yes. Is something like this available with React?" Shawn asked.

"Yes. React allows creating components that are namespaced under a parent component so that they don't interfere with other components or global functions."

"We are using very generic names such as Rows and Headings that can be used later in other parts of the app too. So it makes sense to namespace them now, rather than later." explained Mike.

"Agreed. Let's do it right away," Shawn.

"We need to represent the top-level component as custom component rather than using the `<table>` element."

```
var RecentChangesTable = React.createClass({
    render: function() {
        return <table>
                {this.props.children}
```

```
                </table>;
    }
});
```

"Now, we can replace the `App` component to use `RecentChangesTable` instead of `<table>`."

```
var App = React.createClass({
  render: function(){
    return(<RecentChangesTable>
             <Headings headings = {this.props.headings} />
             <Rows changeSets = {this.props.changeSets} />
           </RecentChangesTable>);
    }
});
```

"Hang on, Mike. We just replaced `<table>` with a custom component. All it does is just render `this.props.children`. How does it get all the headings and rows?" Shawn asked.

"Ah! Nice observation. React, by default, captures all the child nodes between open and close tags of a component in an array and adds it to the props of that component as `this.props.children`. So we can render it using `{this.props.children}`. We will get all Headings and Rows as `this.props.children` in the `RecentChangesTable` component. The output is the same as before, when we used the `<table>` tag directly."

"Awesome!" exclaimed Shawn.

"Cool. Let's move on next step by namespacing all other components under `RecentChangesTable`."

```
RecentChangesTable.Headings = React.createClass({
  render: function() {
    var headings = this.props.headings.map(function(name) {
      return(<RecentChangesTable.Heading heading = {name}/>);
    });

    return (<thead><tr>{headings}</tr></thead>);
  }
});

RecentChangesTable.Heading = React.createClass({
  render: function() {
    return(<th>
```

```
                    {this.props.heading}
             </th>);
   }
});


RecentChangesTable.Row = React.createClass({
  render: function() {
    return(<tr>
             <td>{this.props.changeSet.when}</td>
             <td>{this.props.changeSet.who}</td>
             <td>{this.props.changeSet.description}</td>
         </tr>);
  }
});

RecentChangesTable.Rows = React.createClass({
  render: function() {
    var rows = this.props.changeSets.map(function(changeSet) {
      return(<RecentChangesTable.Row changeSet = {changeSet}/>);
    });

    return (<tbody>{rows}</tbody>);
  }
});
```

"We will also need to update the App component to use namespaced components now."

```
var App = React.createClass({
  render: function(){
    return(<RecentChangesTable>
             <RecentChangesTable.Headings headings = {this.props.
headings} />
             <RecentChangesTable.Rows changeSets = {this.props.
changeSets} />
           </RecentChangesTable>);
    }
});
```

"We are now done. Everything is namespaced under RecentChangesTable now", said Mike.

Spread attributes

Shawn learned a lot of things about JSX but when he was reflecting on the previous steps, he came up with another question.

"Mike, as of now we are just passing two props to the `App` component: `headings` and `changesets`. However, tomorrow these props can increase to any number. Passing them one by one would be cumbersome. Especially, when we have to pass some data from the recent changes API directly. It will be hard to a keep track of the structure of the incoming data and pass it accordingly in the props. Is there a better way?"

"Another excellent question, Shawn. True, it might be cumbersome passing a large number of attributes to the component one by one. But we can solve this using the `spread` attributes."

```
var props = { headings: headings, changeSets: data, timestamps:
timestamps };
ReactDOM.render(<App {...props } />,
                document.getElementById('container'));
```

"In this case, all the properties of object are passed as props to the `App` component. We can pass any object that can contain any number of key value pairs and all of them will be passed as props to the component" explained Mike.

"Very cool. Is the (...) operator present only in JSX?"

"Nope. It is actually based on the spread attribute feature in ES2015, which is the next JavaScript standard. ES2015, or ES6 as it is called, introduces some new features in JavaScript language and React is taking advantage of these developing standards in order to provide a cleaner syntax in JSX" added Mike.

 ES2015 already supports spread operator for arrays at `https://developer.mozilla.org/en-US/docs/Web/JavaScript/Reference/Operators/Spread_operator`. There is also a proposal for objects at `https://github.com/sebmarkbage/ecmascript-rest-spread`.

"Not only this, spread attributes can be used multiple times or it can be combined with other attributes. The order of the attributes is important though. Newer attributes override previous ones."

```
var data = [{ "when": "2 minutes ago",
             "who": "Jill Dupre",
             "description": "Created new account"
           },
           {
```

```
                    "when": "1 hour ago",
                    "who": "Lose White",
                    "description": "Added fist chapter"
                }];
    var headings = ['When', 'Who', 'Description'];

    var props = { headings: headings, changeSets: data };

    ReactDOM.render(<App {...props} headings = {['Updated at ', 'Author',
    'Change']} />, document.getElementById('container'));
```

"Instead of showing **When, Who,** and **Description, Updated at, Author,** and **Change** will be shown as the headings in this case" Mike explained.

Output		Run with JS Auto-run JS ☑ ↗
Updated at	**Author**	**Change**
2 minutes ago	Jill Dupre	Created new account
1 hour ago	Lose White	Added fist chapter

 ES2015 or ES6 is the latest version JavaScript standard. It has a lot of features, which are used by React, similar to the spread attributes. We will be using lot more ES2015 or ES6 code in the upcoming chapters.

Styles in JSX

"Mike, all of the things that we did today are very cool. When do we start adding styles? How can I make this page look pretty? Right now it's a bit dull." Shawn asked.

"Ah, right. Let's do that. React allows us to pass styles to the components the same way props can be passed. For example, we want our headings to be of the floral white color and maybe we want to change the font size. We will represent it in a typical CSS way as follows:"

```
background-color: 'FloralWhite',
font-size: '19px';
```

"We can represent this as a JavaScript object in the CamelCase fashion."

```
var headingStyle = { backgroundColor: 'FloralWhite',
                     fontSize: '19px'
                   };
```

Then, we can use it in each Heading component as a JavaScript object."

```
RecentChangesTable.Heading = React.createClass({
  render: function() {
    var headingStyle = { backgroundColor: 'FloralWhite',
                         fontSize: '19px' };
    return(<th style={headingStyle}>{this.props.heading}</th>);
  }
});
```

"Similarly, let's change the rows to have their own styles."

```
RecentChangesTable.Row = React.createClass({
render: function() {
var trStyle = { backgroundColor: 'aliceblue' };
  return <tr style={trStyle}>
            <td>{this.props.changeSet.when}</td>
            <td>{this.props.changeSet.who}</td>
            <td>{this.props.changeSet.description}</td>
         </tr>;
  }
});
```

"We now have some shiny new headings and rows sprinkled by CSS styling"
Mike added.

Output		Run with JS Auto-run JS
Updated at	**Author**	**Change**
2 minutes ago	Jill Dupre	Created new account
1 hour ago	Lose White	Added fist chapter

"Nice. The name of the attribute to pass these styles must be 'style', right?"
Shawn asked.

"Yes. Also the keys of this style object need to be CamelCased, for example,
backgroundColor, backgroundImage, fontSize, and so on."

"Mike, I understood the inline styling, however, how to add the CSS classes?"

"Ah right. We can pass the class name as an attribute to the DOM tags. Let's extract the styling to a new `recentChangesTable` CSS class."

```
// css
recentChangesTable {
    background-color: 'FloralWhite',
    font-size: '19px'
}
```

"Now, to apply this class to our component, all we need to do is pass it to the component using the expalined `className` prop."

```
render: function(){
    return <table className = 'recentChangesTable'>
                <Headings headings = {this.props.headings} />
                <Rows changeSets = {this.props.changeSets} />
            </table>;
    }
});
```

"As we have seen previously, React makes use of the CamelCase attributes. Here, the `className` prop will be converted to a normal class attribute when React renders the actual HTML."

```
<table class = 'recentChangesTable'>
...
</table>
```

"We can also pass multiple classes to the `className` prop."

```
<table className = 'recentChangesTable userHeadings'>
```

"That's it! We can simply start using the styles freely in our components. This makes it trivial to integrate React with existing CSS styles."

JSX Gotchas

The day was heading to an end. Mike and Shawn were still discussing about this shiny new thing—JSX. Mike decided that it was time to tell Shawn about the issues with using JSX.

"Shawn, so how do you feel about using JSX?"

"I liked it so far. It's very similar to the HTML markup. I can pass attributes, styles, and even classes. I can also use all the DOM elements" explained Shawn.

"Yes. But JSX is not HTML. We have to always remember this. Otherwise, we will run into trouble."

"For example, if you want to pass some custom attribute that does not exist in the HTML specification, then React will simply ignore it."

```
// custom-attribute won't be rendered
<table custom-attribute = 'super_awesome_table'>
</table>
```

"It must be passed as a data attribute so that React will render it."

```
// data-custom-attribute will be rendered
<table data-custom-attribute = 'super_awesome_table'>
</table>
```

"We may also run into some issues while rendering the HTML content dynamically. In the JSX tags, we can add a valid HTML entity directly."

```
// Using HTML entity inside JSX tags.
<div> Mike &amp; Shawn </div>
// will produce
 React.createElement("div", null, " Mike & Shawn ")
```

"But if we render it in a dynamic expression, it will then escape the ampersand."

```
// Using HTML entity inside dynamic expression
var first = 'Mike';
var second = 'Shawn';
<div> { first + '&amp;' + second } </div>

var first = 'Mike';
var second = 'Shawn';
React.createElement("div", null, " ", first + '&amp;' + second, " ")
```

"It happens as React escapes all the strings in order to prevent XSS attacks by default. To overcome it, we can directly pass the Unicode character of & or we can use arrays of strings and JSX elements." Mike explained.

```
// Using mixed arrays of JSX elements and normal variables
<div> {[first, <span>&amp;</span>, second]} </div>

React.createElement("div", null, " ", [first,
                                    React.createElement("span", null,
    "&"), second], " ")
```

"Wow. It can get pretty messed up" expressed Shawn.

"Well, yes, but if we remember the rules, then it's pretty simple. Also, as a last resort, React also allows to render raw HTML using a special `dangerouslySetInnerHTML` prop."

```
// Rendering raw HTML directly
<div dangerouslySetInnerHTML={{__html: 'Mike &amp; Shawn'}} />
```

"Although this option should be used after consideration about what is getting rendered to prevent XSS attacks" Mike explained.

Conditionals in JSX

"React embraces the idea of tying markup and logic that generates the markup together. This means that we can use the power of JavaScript for loops and conditionals."

"But if/else logic is a bit hard to express in markup. Therefore, in JSX, we can't use conditional statements such as if/else."

```
// Using if/else directly doesn't work
<div className={if(success) { 'green' } else { 'red' }}/>
Error: Parse Error: Line 1: Unexpected token if
```

"Instead, we can use a ternary operator for specifying the if/else logic."

```
// Using ternary operator
<div className={ success ? 'green' : 'red' }/>
React.createElement("div", {className:  success ? 'green' : 'red'})
```

"But ternary operator gets cumbersome with large expressions when we want to use the React component as a child. In this case, it's better to offload the logic to a block or maybe a function" Mike added.

```
// Moving if/else logic to a function
var showResult = function() {
  if(this.props.success === true)
    return <SuccessComponent />
  else
    return <ErrorComponent />
};
```

Non-DOM attributes

"Alright Shawn, it's time to take a detailed look at our application again. If you closely see the console output, you will see a few warnings related to Keys."

```
"Each child in an array should have a unique \"key\" prop. Check the
render method of Rows. See http://fb.me/react-warning-keys for more
information."
```

"In the `render()` method of Rows, we are rendering collection of the Row components."

```
RecentChangesTable.Rows = React.createClass({
  render: function() {
    var rows = this.props.changeSets.map(function(changeSet) {
      return(<Row changeSet = {changeSet}/>);
    });

    return <tbody>{rows}</tbody>;
  }
});
```

"During the rendering of list items, a component may move up or down in the DOM tree based on the user interaction. For example, in case of search or sorting, the items in the list can change their position. New items can also get added to the front of the list in case new data gets fetched. In such cases, React may remove and recreate components based on the diff algorithm. But if we provide a unique identifier for each element in the list, then React will intelligently decide whether to destroy it or not. This will improve the rendering performance. This can be achieved by passing a unique `key` prop to every item in the list."

In our case, the number of rows is currently fixed. But later on, we want to show the updates page as the new data is being fetched from the API. The situation gets complicated when children are added or removed dynamically as the state and identity of each component must be maintained in every render pass. The `key` prop will help React to uniquely identify the component in such cases. Go ahead and use the index of the Row component for this purpose as it will be unique as of now" Mike further explained.

"Cool. So let me try adding the `key` prop to Rows. I noticed same issue with the `Headings` component too, therefore, I will add a key for `Headings` as well." said Shawn.

```
RecentChangesTable.Rows = React.createClass({
  render: function() {
```

```
        var rows = this.props.changeSets.map(function(changeSet, index) {
          return(<Row key={index} changeSet = {changeSet}/>);
        });

        return (<div>{rows}</div>);
    }
});
RecentChangesTable.Headings = React.createClass({
    render: function() {
        var headings = this.props.headings.map(function(name, index) {
          return(<RecentChangesTable.Heading key={index} heading =
{name}/>);
        });

        return (<thead><tr>{headings}</tr></thead>);
    }
});
```

"Perfect. Note that the value of keys for a given list should be unique. We will get to know more about the keys when we start updating the DOM based on dynamic data. But this is good enough for now" said Mike.

"Makes sense. Are there any more such keywords/identifiers available for us?"

"Yes. Along with key, there is also refs or references. It allows the parent component to keep a reference of a child component. Right now, we can't access the child components outside the `render()` method of the component. But having `ref` allows us to use the child component anywhere in the component, not just the `render()` method."

```
<input ref="myInput" />
```

"Now, we can access these references outside the render method too."

```
this.refs.myInput
```

"It's pretty useful when we want to inform a component to change something at runtime. We will discuss and use `refs` in more detail later when we deal with event handlers" Mike added.

Summary

In this chapter, we dived deep into JSX. We discussed why using JSX makes development with React easy and how JSX gets transformed into the plain native JavaScript. We split big the single React component into small, focused components and understood the advantages of reusable, modular components. We saw different JSX tags, JavaScript expressions, and how React is taking advantages of ES6 features such as spread attributes. In the end, we discussed advanced topics such as namespaced components and some gotchas that we should keep in mind while using JSX.

In the next chapter, we will focus on data flow and models to access data and component life cycle and their use.

3
Data Flow and Life Cycle Events

In the previous chapter, we saw the power of JSX. JSX makes it easy to write the React components.

In this chapter, we will focus on the data flow between components and how to manage state and life cycle of components.

In this chapter, we will cover the following points:

- Data flow in React
- Props
- PropTypes
- State
- State versus props
- When to use state and props
- Component life cycle overview
- Component life cycle methods

At the end of the chapter, we will get familiar with the data flow in the React components and the ways of maintaining and managing state. We will also get used to the life cycle of a component and various life cycle hooks provided by React.

Data flow in React

Shawn and Mark were getting ready to start working on a rainy day with a cup of coffee.

"Hey Mike, I have a question about props that we used to pass the `headings` and `changeSet` data to other components."

"Shoot!" Mike exclaimed.

"It seems to me that we are passing data to the components that are below the current component, but how can a component pass the data to the parent component?"

"Ah. In React, by default, all the data flows only in one direction: from parent component to child component. That's it."

This makes the job of the child component simple and predictable. Take props from the parent and render." Mike explained.

```
var RecentChangesTables = React.createClass({
  render: function(){
    return(<table className = 'table'>
              <Headings headings = {this.props.headings} />
              <Rows changeSets = {this.props.changeSets} />
           </table>);
    }
});
```

"Let's look at our example. The `RecentChangesTables` component passes the props to the `Headings` and `Rows` components. So basically, we can say that `RecentChangesTables` owns the `Headings` and `Rows` components."

"In React, an owner component sets props for another components." Mike explained.

"Got it. Therefore, in the preceding case, `<table>` is also owned by `RecentChangesTables`?" Shawn asked.

"No. The owner relationship is specific to the React components. In this case, table is the parent of `Headings` and `Rows`, similar to the parent-child relationship in DOM. But it's not an owner of them." explained Mike.

"A component is the owner of a child component if that child gets created in the render method of the parent. I guess this will solve the confusion." Mike added.

"Yes. Got the difference between owner and parent-child relationship." said Shawn.

"Furthermore, a component should not mutate its props. They should always be consistent with what the parent has set. It's a very important point that makes React's behavior consistent as well as fast, as we'll see soon." Mike further added.

"Props can be accessed by this.props, as we have already seen. If anything in the parent's props changes, React will make sure that the changes are flown downstream and will re-render the component tree." Mike.

"Excellent. Yesterday, I was reading something about validating the props." remembered Shawn.

"Yes. React allows validating the props using PropTypes. Let's take a look at them." said Mike, taking a sip from his freshly ground coffee.

Props validation

"React provides a way to validate the props using PropTypes. This is extremely useful to ensure that the components are used correctly. Here is an example of using propTypes for our app." explained Mike.

```
var App = React.createClass({
  propTypes: {
   headings: React.PropTypes.array,
   changeSets: React.PropTypes.array,
   author: React.PropTypes.string.isRequired
   },

  render: function(){
    return(<table className = 'table'>
            <Headings headings = {this.props.headings} />
            <Rows changeSets = {this.props.changeSets} />
          </table>);
    }
});
```

"Oh! Will it show an error as we are not passing the author, which is required, I assume? I see that `propTypes` has set the author value to be `isRequired`." Shawn asked.

Console

"Warning: Required prop `author` was not specified in `App`."

"No. It will not throw an error, but it will show a nice warning for us to take a look at." said Mike.

"Also, `propTypes` are only checked in development. Their job is to just check that all the assumptions that we are making about our components are being met." Mike added.

"Got it. I agree that it's better to have it rather than getting surprised by random hiccups during production," Shawn.

"Yes. It's especially useful as, along with standard types, we can also validate the custom types." Mike informed.

```
var App = React.createClass({
  propTypes: {
    headings: function(props, propName, componentName) {
    if(propName === 'headings')
      return Error('Failed Validation');
    }
  },

  render: function(){
    return(<table className = 'table'>
            <Headings headings = {this.props.headings} />
            <Rows changeSets = {this.props.changeSets} />
          </table>);
    }
});
```

"Therefore, if the structure of the props is not as per your assumption, you can raise a warning by defining a custom validator as shown in the previous case", Mike explained.

Specifying default props

"Shawn, React also allows us to define some default values for props. This is useful when parent component is passing props based on some condition or not passing some props at all due to some change," Mike said.

```
var App = React.createClass({

  getDefaultProps: function() {
    return {
      headings: ['When happened ', 'Who did it', 'What they change']
    };
  },

  render: function(){
          ...
  }
});

var data = [{ "when": "2 minutes ago",
              "who": "Jill Dupre",
              "description": "Created new account"
            },
            {
              "when": "1 hour ago",
              "who": "Lose White",
              "description": "Added first chapter"
            }];

React.render(<App changeSets={data}/>, document.body);
```

"Here, we updated the code to not send the headings from props. Instead, we used the `getDefaultProps` function to define the default props that will be used in case they are not passed."

Output		Run with JS Auto-run JS ↗
When happened	**Who did it**	**What they change**
2 minutes ago	Jill Dupre	Created new account
1 hour ago	Lose White	Added first chapter

"Therefore, our output looks like this."

"Oh, ok. Makes sense. Rather than fiddling with the if-else clauses to check whether the prop is present, default props make it simple enough to predefine our data." said Shawn.

Modifying this.props.children

"Shawn. There is one special prop that we should know about. It's this.props. children," continued Mike.

"React captures all the children that are present in the opening and closing tag into props that can be accessed through this.props.children." said Mike.

"Let's try to modify our code to use this.props.children. This is also required as we want to display a header for our output table." Mike added.

```
var RecentChangesTable = React.createClass({
  render: function(){
          return(
          <div>
            <h1> Recent Changes </h1>
            <table className='table'>
               {this.props.children}
            </table>
          </div>
          );
  }
});

var App = React.createClass({
  render: function(){
     return(<RecentChangesTable>
              <Headings headings = {this.props.headings} />
              <Rows changeSets = {this.props.changeSets} />
            </RecentChangesTable>);
     }
});
```

Output		Run with JS Auto-run JS ↗

Recent Changes

Updated at	Author	Change
2 minutes ago	Jill Dupre	Created new account
1 hour ago	Lose White	Added first chapter

"Cool. So we extracted the table in its own component and also added a header."
Shawn confirmed.

"Yes and we rendered `Headings` and `Rows` using `this.props.children`."
Mike explained.

"Awesome. Let me change our code based on our discussion about props."
Shawn said excitedly.

State

"Shawn, let's talk about one more technique of handling data in a component, state.
Every component can have its own state in React. The main difference between state
and props is that props are passed to the component from the parent component;
whereas, state is something that is internal to the component.

Props are passed when a component gets instantiated. State is something that can
change over time. Therefore, changes in state affect the rendering of components.
Consider state as some sort of private data structure of the component." Mike added.

"Mike, but then we have not used state at all until now. We were just using props."
Shawn asked.

"True. That is because state should be introduced only when it is required. You
already know managing state is hard. As we were playing with static data of
`ChangeSets` API, we didn't require state. However, we will need it very soon."
Mike added.

Setting initial state

"The initial state can be set using the `getInitialState` function." said Mike.

```
var App = React.createClass({
  getInitialState: function() {
    return {
      changeSets: []
    };
  },

  render: function(){
    console.log(this.state.changeSets); // prints []
});
```

"State can be accessed similar to props using `this.state`." Mike explained further.

Setting state

"We might need to update the initial state based on some user events. Updating state is also easy using the `setState()` function." informed Mike.

```
var App = React.createClass({
  getInitialState: function() {
    return {
      changeSets: [],
      headings: ['Updated At', 'Author', 'Change']
    };
  },

  handleEvent: function(data) {
    this.setState({ changeSets: data.changeSets });
  },

  render: function(){
    ...
});
```

Avoiding state

"Currently, we don't need state; however, when we fetch the dynamic data from `RecentChanges` API, we will use state with props." Mike added.

"Cool. Based on our discussion, I think that we should avoid state as much as possible." Shawn suggested.

"True. If a component does not change, then there is no need to use state. It's better to depend on props passed by the parent component in that case. This also avoids re-rendering of the component again and again as changes to state initiate a re-render of the component." Mike explained.

State versus props

"Shawn, it's important to understand the difference between props and state and where to use what." informed Mike.

"Props are immutable. They should not be updated by the component to which they are passed. They are are owned by the component which passes them to some other component. State is something internal and private to the component. State can and will change depending on the interactions with the outer world." said Mike.

"State should store as simple data as possible, such as whether an input checkbox is checked or not or a CSS class that hides or displays the component." Mike added.

"Another thing to make sure is to not duplicate props in state." said Mike.

```
var App = React.createClass({
  getInitialState: function() {
    return {
      changeSets: this.props.changeSets
    };
  }
});
```

"It is possible to set the state based on data passed in props. However, the parent component can update the props and send them again. In this case, the state will be muddled up with new data if there have been any changes to the state."

"Also, the data is present at two places now, therefore, it becomes harder to manage two sources of data." Mike explained.

"I think that in such cases, it's best to use props directly, right?" Shawn asked.

"Yes. The state is entirely optional. It's best to avoid it as much as possible. You got that right." Mike said happily.

Component life cycle overview

"Shawn, now let's start taking a look at how to dynamically fetch data from `https://openlibrary.org/`, store it in our component, and render it after making it compatible to render.

A component goes through different life cycle events. They help facilitate when we should initialize which part of a component or when should some external data be fetched.

We have already seen some of these methods such as `render`, `getInitialState`, and `getDefaultProps`.

An updated detailed list and example for the same can be found at `http://videos.bigbinary.com/react/react-life-cycle-methods-in-depth.html`.

Let's go through each of these, one by one, and how they can be used so that we can start fetching dynamic information for display. Here is a list of methods that we will discuss:

- `componentWillMount`
- `componentDidMount`
- `componentWillReceiveProps(object nextProps)`
- `boolean shouldComponentUpdate(object nextProps, object nextState)`
- `componentWillUpdate(object nextProps, object nextState)`
- `componentDidUpdate(object prevProps, object prevState)`
- `componentWillUnmount()`
- `React.unmountComponentAtNode(document.body)`

You can follow along the next example at `http://jsbin.com/tijeco/3/edit`.

Component life cycle methods

"Shawn, let's start with an exhaustive example that triggers these methods." Mike informed.

```javascript
console.log('Start') // Marks entry point of JS code.
var App = React.createClass({
    componentWillMount: function(){
      console.log('componentWillMount');
    },

    componentDidMount: function(){
      console.log('componentDidMount');
    },

    getInitialState: function(){
      return { status: true}
    },

    getDefaultProps: function(){
      return {name: 'John'};
    },

    componentWillReceiveProps: function(nextProps){
      console.log('componentWillReceiveProps');
    },

    shouldComponentUpdate: function(nextProps, nextState){
      console.log('shouldComponentUpdate');
      return true;
    },

    componentWillUpdate: function(){
      console.log('componentWillUpdate');
    },

    render: function() {
      console.log('render');
      return <h1 onClick={this.toggleState}>
            {this.state.status.toString()}
            </h1>
    },

    componentWillUnmount: function(){
```

```
        console.log('componentWillUnmount')
      },

      toggleState: function() {
        this.setState({status: !this.state.status})
      }
      });

   /* List of methods and signatures for reference
    * componentWillMount
    * componentDidMount
    * componentWillReceiveProps(object nextProps)
    * boolean shouldComponentUpdate(object nextProps, object nextState)
    * componentWillUpdate(object nextProps, object nextState)
    * componentDidUpdate(object prevProps, object prevState)
    * componentWillUnmount()
    /

   React.render(<App name='Jane'/>, document.body);
```

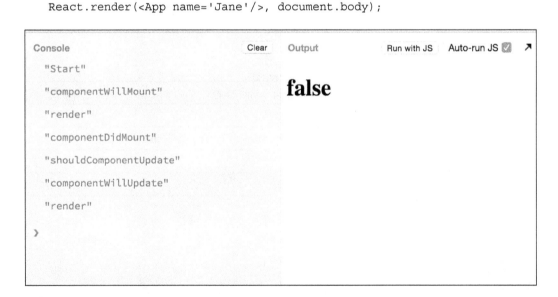

"It simply displays a body with the `true` text and then on clicking, it changes it to display `false`." Mike.

"Shawn, to keep things simple, I have added just a simple `console.log()` method for every life cycle method so that we know it was called. If we do a fresh run, the following is printed:"

```
"Start"
"componentWillMount"
"render"
"componentDidMount"
```

"Ah, got it. Basically, the window first printed `Start` to signal the file has been loaded." Shawn said.

"Correct. Next, it printed out `componentWillMount`. That's the entry point for our component. This method is called when a component gets mounted on the body for the first time. If you can see, we are calling `React.render`."

```
React.render(<App name='Jane'/>, document.body);
```

This is what triggers `componentWillMount`. In this method, we can call `setState` to perform some changes to our internal data. However, that doesn't call a new re-render or this method again.

Next is the actual `render` method call. This is responsible for the actual component display.

Finally, we have a call to `componentDidMount`. This is invoked immediately after mounting the component and only once after the component is rendered.

We can make use of this to fetch the dynamic information that we want to display in our component after the initial render of the component.

"Once that's done, we are done with our initial run for the display of a component!"

"Nice." exclaimed Shawn.

"Now, we have added a simple `onClick` event. This calls `this.toggleState`, which toggles the current status from `true` to `false` and vice versa."

As the state is affected, React re-renders the `App` component. We can see the method call sequence when this happens, as follows:"

```
"..."
"shouldComponentUpdate"
"componentWillUpdate"
"render"
"..."
```

"Ah, nice. It went through another re-render cycle." said Shawn.

"Correct. When the state was changed, React knew it needed to re-render the App component. It calls shouldComponentUpdate first. This method returns true or false indicating React to render the component or not.

"We can also control whether the component should be re-rendered or not even if the state gets updated. This method can return false and then React will not re-render the component even if the state is changed."

```
shouldComponentUpdate: function(nextProps, nextState){
    console.log('shouldComponentUpdate');
    return false; // Will not re-render the component.
},
```

"We can also compare nextProps and nextState to the existing values and then decide whether to re-render."

"Awesome, this means that we could get faster components!" Shawn exclaimed.

"Exactly. By default, it always returns true, to always render on changes."
Mike concluded.

"Next up, componentWillUpdate will get called just before rendering. We can take care of any changes that we would like to do or any housekeeping. One thing to note is that we can't call setState in this method. State updates should be handled elsewhere."

"Oh, ok," Shawn.

"We are only left with componentWillReceiveProps."

```
componentWillReceiveProps: function(nextProps){
    console.log('componentWillReceiveProps');
},
```

"It receives nextProps, which are the new props that the child component receives from the parent component. This method is not called for initial render. We can update the state or do some other housekeeping work based on the changes in props."

"Nice, Mike. I think I am getting a better hang of this."

"Finally, we have componentWillUnmount. This is called when the component is unmounted from the body. We can use this to release the resources, perform cleanups, unset any timers, and so on."

"Got it."

"Alright! Let's update our component to start fetching the information from `https://openlibrary.org/`."

"So, what we will be doing is updating the `componentDidMount` to perform an AJAX call and fetch data to display."

```
componentDidMount : function(){
  $.ajax({
    url: 'http://openlibrary.org/recentchanges.json?limit=10',
    context: this,
    dataType: 'json',
    type: 'GET'
  }).done(function (data) {
    var changeSets = this.mapOpenLibraryDataToChangeSet(data);
    this.setState({changeSets: changeSets});
  });
}
```

"Here, we are making a call to `http://openlibrary.org/recentchanges.json?limit=10` and asking for the ten most-recent changes. We will get the data in the following format:"

```
[{
      comment:    "Added new cover",
      kind:       "add-cover",
      author:     {
          key: "/people/fsrc"
      },
      timestamp: "2015-05-25T19:20:33.981700",
      changes:    [
                     {
                         key:        "/books/OL25679864M",
                         revision: 2
                     }
                   ],
      ip:         null,
      data:       { url: "" },
      id:         "49441324"
  },
  {
  ...
  }
  ]
```

"We will need to format the data as per our requirements so that it's displayed nicely. Let's take a look at it:"

```
mapOpenLibraryDataToChangeSet : function (data) {
  return data.map(function (change, index) {
    return {
      "when": jQuery.timeago(change.timestamp),
      "who": change.author.key,
      "description": change.comment
    }
  });
}
```

"Here, we are extracting the timestamp, author information, and description of the change, which is the comment in the change. As the changed time is a timestamp, we have made use of the jQuery.timeago plugin to get desirable display of time, such as 2 minutes ago and so forth. To use this plugin, we need to include it in our HTML head tag." Mike explained.

```
<script src="jquery.timeago.js" type="text/javascript"></script>
```

"Looks like it's all coming together." Shawn.

"It is, let's take a look at everything in action, shall we?"

```
var Heading = React.createClass({
    render: function () {
        var headingStyle = {
            backgroundColor: 'FloralWhite',
            fontSize: '19px'
        };
        return (<th style={headingStyle}> {this.props.heading} </th>);
    }
});
var Headings = React.createClass({
    render: function () {
        var headings = this.props.headings.map(function (name, index)
{
            return (<Heading key={"heading-" + index}
heading={name}/>);
        });

        return (<tr className='table-th'> {headings} </tr>);
    }
});
```

```
var Row = React.createClass({
    render: function () {
        var trStyle = {backgroundColor: 'aliceblue'};
        return (<tr style={trStyle}>
            <td> {this.props.changeSet.when} </td>
            <td> {this.props.changeSet.who} </td>
            <td> {this.props.changeSet.description} </td>
        </tr>);
    }
});
var Rows = React.createClass({
    render: function () {
        var rows = this.props.changeSets.map(function (changeSet,
index) {
            return (<Row key={index} changeSet={changeSet}/>);
        });

        return (<tbody>{rows}</tbody>);
    }
});


var App = React.createClass({
    getInitialState: function () {
        return {changeSets: [];
    },
    mapOpenLibraryDataToChangeSet: function (data) {
        return data.map(function (change, index) {
            return {
                "when": jQuery.timeago(change.timestamp),
                "who": change.author.key,
                "description": change.comment
            }
        });
    },
    componentDidMount: function () {
        $.ajax({
            url: 'http://openlibrary.org/recentchanges.json?limit=10',
            context: this,
            dataType: 'json',
            type: 'GET'
        }).done(function (data) {
            var changeSets = this.mapOpenLibraryDataToChangeSet(data);
            this.setState({changeSets: changeSets});
        });
```

```
        },

    render: function () {
        return (<table className='table'>
            <Headings headings={this.props.headings}/>
            <Rows changeSets={this.state.changeSets}/>
        </table>);
    }
});

var headings = ['Updated at ', 'Author', 'Change'];
React.render(<App headings={headings} />, document.body);
```

"Here's our final product!", exclaimed Mike.

"Awesome, I can't wait to see what we build next!" Shawn added.

Another productive day at Adequate. Mike and Shawn, happy with the progress, headed back.

Summary

In this chapter, we looked at how to pass around data in the React components using props and state. We also discussed how and when to use state and props. We looked at how `propTypes` can be used to validate the props. After that, we discussed the component's life cycle. We discussed about the various life cycle methods and how they can be used. After that, we used these life cycle methods to get real-time data from Open Library API.

4

Composite Dynamic Components and Forms

In the previous chapter, we saw the various life cycle methods of a React component, how the data flows between React components, and how to manage state and props in our React application.

In this chapter, we will focus on multiple dynamic components and building forms using React.

We will cover following points:

- Multiple dynamic components with interactivity
- Controlled and uncontrolled components
- Form elements
- Form events and handlers

At the end of this chapter, we will be able to create applications containing complex forms using React with an understanding of the dynamic components.

Mike and Shawn are getting ready for their next project. The application is a prototype for an online bookstore where people can buy different books. Shawn is excited to work with Mike again and learn more about React. This project is based on React too.

Forms in React

"Shawn, in this project there will be many things related to placing an order, taking user's shipping and billing information, and so on. We are going to deal with a lot of forms now." started Mike.

"Forms using React, right?" Shawn asked excitedly.

"Yes. That is why today we will only focus on forms. Let's go through the intrinsic details of using forms using React." said Mike.

Setting up the application

"Shawn, we were using JSBin up to this point. But now we will create the app locally. We will use the following directory structure for our code:"

```
$ tree -L 1
.
├── LICENSE
├── README.md
├── index.html
├── node_modules
├── package.json
├── server.js
├── src
└── webpack.config.js

2 directories, 6 files
```

- The `src` directory will contain all of the React components
- The `webpack.config.js` and `server.js` file will be used for setting up local development server using webpack.
- The `package.json` file will be used to contain information about all of the npm packages used by us
- The `index.html` file will be the starting point of the app

"Let's see our `index.html` file."

```html
// index.html
<html>
  <head>
    <title>Forms in React</title>
    <link rel="stylesheet"  href="https://maxcdn.bootstrapcdn.com/
bootstrap/3.3.5/css/bootstrap.min.css" />
  </head>
```

```
  <body>
    <div id='root' class="container">
    </div>
  </body>
  <script src="/static/bundle.js"></script>
</html>
```

"We are using bootstrap CSS to beautify our app. Other than this, we are including the bundled JavaScript as `static/bundle.js`. Webpack will bundle the JavaScript code from our app and place it in `static/bundle.js`."

 Webpack is a module bundler that takes our JavaScript code and generates static assets representing these modules. It also has other features such as hot module replacement, which we will be using in this book. We will be covering webpack and it's configuration in more depth in *Chapter 11, React Tools*.

"Let's see our `index.js` file, which will be the entry point of the JavaScript code."

```
// src/index.js

import ReactDOM from 'react-dom';
import BookStore from './BookStore';

ReactDOM.render(<BookStore />, document.getElementById('root'));
```

"It will render our `BookStore` component in the root container present in `index.html`. Now, the only thing left to do is actually writing the code for our `BookStore` component. Let's get started."

"Mike, in JSBin, our ES6 code was getting converted to normal JavaScript automatically. How will it be converted now?" asked Shawn.

"Excellent question. I forgot to mention about using Babel. Babel is a JavaScript transpiler that will convert our ES6 and JSX code to normal JavaScript. I have already configured this app to use Babel. You can check `package.json` and `webpack.config.js` to see how we configured Babel to convert the ES6 code to ES5 code. But let's not worry too much about it for now. We will come back to it and see how the whole setup works later."

We will be covering how we have used Babel and Webpack in *Chapter 11, React Tools*. Right now, the reader is expected to not worry about it and directly set up the application using the instructions given in source code of this chapter. You can also check *Chapter 11, React Tools* for more details before completing this chapter.

Getting started with forms

"Forms behave slightly differently in the React world than in the normal HTML world. They are a bit special than the other DOM components in the React world. The <input>, <textarea>, and <option> tags are some of the common input components provided by React." explained Mike.

"These form components are mutated when the user interacts with them, adds some text in the input, or selects an option. Therefore, we need to take care that we are managing those user interactions properly." Mike explained further.

"Let's start with a simple input tag to understand the user interaction." informed Mike.

```
// src/index.js

import React from 'react';
import ReactDOM from 'react-dom';

var InputExample = React.createClass({
  render() {
    return (
      <input type="text" value="Shawn" />
    );
  }
});
ReactDOM.render(<InputExample />,
                document.getElementById('root'));
```

"Mike, what is the meaning of import here?" asked Shawn.

"Good catch. This is one of the ES6 features that we are going to use in this project. It is used to import functions defined in other modules or external scripts."

More information on import can be found at https://developer. mozilla.org/en/docs/web/javascript/reference/ statements/import.

"We are also using a new way of defining functions in ES6."

```
// Old way of defining function
render: function() {
  return (
    <input type="text" value="Shwn" />
  );
}

// New way of defining function
render() {
    return (
      <input type="text" value="Shawn" />
    );
  }
```

"Using this new syntax, we don't have to write word `function` every time we define the function."

"Shawn, start our app by running `npm start`."

$ npm start

> reactjs-by-example-react-forms@0.0.1 start /Users/prathamesh/Projects/ sources/reactjs-by-example/chapter4

> node server.js

Listening at localhost:9000

Hash: 8ec0d12965567260413b

Version: webpack 1.9.11

Time: 1639ms

"Awesome, it works because we have configured the `package.json` scripts section for starting the app."

```
// package.json
......
"scripts": {
  "start": "node server.js",
  "lint": "eslint src"
},
......
```

"Let's get back to our input box. We see a normal HTML text input with a predefined value, Shawn. All good." said Mike.

"Mike, I can't edit it. Seems like the field is read-only. Also, I am seeing a warning in the console." informed Shawn.

```
⚠ 2015-06-24 16:42:40.254 Warning: Failed propType: You provided a `value` prop to a    warning.js:48
  form field without an `onChange` handler. This will render a read-only field. If the field should
  be mutable use `defaultValue`. Otherwise, set either `onChange` or `readOnly`. Check the render
  method of `InputExample`.
```

Interactive props

"Right. It also says that value is a prop. Similar to value, there are some other props supported by the input fields." said Mike.

- value
- defaultValue
- onChange

"As React has warned us that we need to either provide the defaultValue or onChange prop to make this field mutable, let's take care of this and add a onChange handler. The field is read-only because by setting the value prop, we have rendered a controlled component." explained Mike.

Controlled components

"What is a controlled component, Mike?" asked Shawn.

"It's an input component whose value is controlled by React. By providing the value prop, we are informing React that the value of this field is "Shawn". Once React has declared it to be "Shawn", any user input won't have an effect as the value is already set in the ." explained Mike.

"I think that we have to resort to state instead of props?" Shawn asked.

"Exactly. As an user is interacting with the input field, we need to update the value prop using state and onChange event handler. Can you give it a try?" suggested Mike.

```
// src/index.js

var InputExample = React.createClass({
  getInitialState() {
    return (
      { name: '-'}
    );
  },

  handleChange(event) {
    this.setState({ name: event.target.value });
  },

  render() {
    return (
      <input type="text"
             value={this.state.name}
             onChange={this.handleChange} />
    );
  }
});
```

"Awesome. This pattern of making the value of an input based on state and updating the state based on the user interaction makes it very easy to respond to user interactions. We can also do some housekeeping things such as validating the input." Mike explained further.

"For example, you can change the case of all the text to uppercase." Mike added.

```
handleChange: function(event) {
  this.setState({name: event.target.value.toUpperCase()});
}
```

Uncontrolled components

"React also has uncontrolled components where the `value` prop is not passed to the input".

```
render() {
    return (
      <input type="text" />
    );
  }
```

"In this case, the value entered by the user will be immediately reflected in the input. For setting some default initial value, we can pass the default `value` prop, which will act as the initial value for an uncontrolled component."

```
render() {
    return (
      <input type="text" defaultValue="Shawn"/>
    );
  }
```

"Awesome. This does it."

Getting started with form wizard

"Shawn, our task today is to build a form wizard, modeling all the steps that the user will take while using the online bookstore."

- We will start with a form, where the user selects the book that they want to buy
- In the next step, the user will enter the information related to the billing and shipping address
- After this, the user needs to choose a delivery mechanism
- In the end, the user will confirm the transaction and place the order

"Will we design four different forms then?" asked Shawn.

"Yes. But all of them will be controlled by a single parent. The parent component will keep a track of the state that the user is in and will render a form for this step." explained Mike.

```js
// src/BookStore.js

import React from 'react';

var BookStore = React.createClass({
  render() {
    switch (step) {
      case 1:
        return <BookList />;
      case 2:
        return <ShippingDetails />;
      case 3:
        return <DeliveryDetails />;
    }
  }
});
```

"How will we control the step?" asked Shawn.

"We will discuss this point later. Let's fill in some details before that. Let's add the placeholders for all of our forms." said Mike.

```js
// src/BookStore.js


var BookList = React.createClass({
  render() {
    return(
      <h1>
        Choose from wide variety of books available in our store.
      </h1>
    );
  }
});

var ShippingDetails = React.createClass({
  render() {
    return(
      <h1>Enter your shipping information.</h1>
    );
  }
```

```
  });

  var DeliveryDetails = React.createClass({
    render() {
      return (
        <h1>Choose your delivery options here.</h1>
      );
    }
  });
```

"Great. Now, let's make sure that we always start from the first step." explained Mike.

```
  // src/BookStore.js

  ......

  var BookStore = React.createClass({
    getInitialState() {
      return ({ currentStep: 1 });
    },

    render() {
      switch (this.state.currentStep) {
        case 1:
          return <BookList />;
        case 2:
          return <ShippingDetails />;
        case 3:
          return <DeliveryDetails />;
      }
    }
  ......

  });
```

"Now that we have made sure that the user will always be on the first step at the start, let's go ahead and finish the book store." said Mike.

```
  // src/BookStore.js

  var BookList = React.createClass({
    getInitialState() {
      return (
        { books: [
```

```
              { name: 'Zero to One', author: 'Peter Thiel' },
              { name: 'Monk who sold his Ferrari', author: 'Robin Sharma' },
              { name: 'Wings of Fire', author: 'A.P.J. Abdul Kalam' }
          ] }
        )
      },

    _renderBook(book) {
      return(
        <div className="checkbox">
          <label>
            <input type="checkbox" /> {book.name} -- {book.author}
          </label>
        </div>
      );
    },

    render() {
      return(
        <div>
          <h3> Choose from wide variety of books available in our store
    </h3>
          <form>
            {this.state.books.map((book) => {
              return this._renderBook(book); })
            }

            <input type="submit" className="btn btn-success" />
          </form>
        </div>
      );
    }
  });
```

"This is our static form. It doesn't do anything on user interaction. The next step will be to make it respond to the events." Mike added.

"Cool, I am interested in how we move to the next step." said Shawn.

"We will reach there soon. Let's finish other things first." informed Mike.

"OK. Before that, what's happening here?"

```
  this.state.books.map((book) => { return (this._renderBook(book)) })
```

"This is called as a **fat arrow syntax** to define functions. It is another ES6 feature. It's a shorthand for writing functions."

 More details about fat arrow functions can be found at
`https://developer.mozilla.org/en/docs/Web/`
`JavaScript/Reference/Functions/Arrow_functions`.

Form events

"Let's handle submitting the form now. React provides the `onSubmit` event for this purpose." said Mike.

```
// src/BookStore.js
......
// Updating BookStore component

render() {
    return(
      <div>
        <h3> Choose from wide variety of books available in our store
</h3>
        <form onSubmit={this.handleSubmit}>
          {this.state.books.map((book) => { return (this._
renderBook(book)) })}

          <input type="submit" className="btn btn-success" />
        </form>
      </div>
    );
  },

handleSubmit(event) {
    console.log(event);
    event.preventDefault();
    console.log("Form submitted");
  }
  ......
```

"Now, the next task is to get hold of all the books selected by the user. We can use state to achieve this." explained Mike.

```js
// src/BookStore.js
......

// Updating BookStore component

getInitialState() {
    return (
      { books: [
        { id: 1, name: 'Zero to One', author: 'Peter Thiel' },
        { id: 2, name: 'Monk who sold his Fearrary', author: 'Robin
Sharma' },
        { id: 3, name: 'Wings of Fire', author: 'A.P.J. Abdul Kalam' }
      ],
        selectedBooks: []
      }
    );
  },

_renderBook(book) {
    return (
      <div className="checkbox" key={book.id}>
        <label>
          <input type="checkbox" value={book.name}
                  onChange={this.handleSelectedBooks}/>
          {book.name} -- {book.author}
        </label>
      </div>
    );
  },

handleSelectedBooks(event) {
    var selectedBooks = this.state.selectedBooks;
    var index = selectedBooks.indexOf(event.target.value);

    if (event.target.checked) {
      if (index === -1)
        selectedBooks.push(event.target.value);
    } else {
      selectedBooks.splice(index, 1);
    }

    this.setState({selectedBooks: selectedBooks });
  }
```

"We added an `onChange` handler for the checkboxes. We also provided the `value` prop to the checkboxes which will be name of the book. Initially, the `selectedBooks` state will be an empty array set through the `getInitialState` function. The `handleSelectedBooks` method will check whether the checkbox is checked or not. We are using the checked prop provided by React for checkbox inputs. Similar to value, it also gets updated with user interaction.

At the end, we are updating the state with the new value of `selectedBooks`. Therefore, at any point of time, we will have hold of selected books in `this.state. selectedBooks`." explained Mike.

"Perfect!" said Shawn.

Parent Child relationship

"Now after this, the next step is communicating with the parent component. Currently, there is no way that our child component can communicate with props. We want to communicate with the parent component as we want to send the selected books by the user to the parent component. The easiest way for a child to communicate with the parent is via props." Mike explained.

"But props are generally the attributes or properties that are sent to a child, right? How can a child communicate with the parent using them?" Shawn asked.

"Remember the {} syntax. We can pass any valid expression as prop. We can pass a function callback as prop to a child component. A child can call it to update the state of the parent. Let's update our `BookStore` component now." Mike explained.

```
// src/BookStore.js

......
// Updating BookStore component

  updateFormData(formData) {
    console.log(formData);
  },

  render() {
    switch (this.state.currentStep) {
      case 1:
        return <BookList
                updateFormData={this.updateFormData} />;
      case 2:
        return <ShippingDetails
```

```
                      updateFormData={this.updateFormData} />;
        case 3:
          return <DeliveryDetails
                      updateFormData={this.updateFormData} />;
      }
    }
    ......

});
```

"We pass the updateFormData function as a prop to all the child components. This function will take care of updating the form data. We will also need to update BookList in order to use it."

```
// src/BookStore.js
// Updating BookList component

......
    handleSubmit(event) {
      event.preventDefault();

      this.props.updateFormData({ selectedBooks:
                                  this.state.selectedBooks });
    }
    ......
});
```

"The BookList component now calls the updateFormData function and passes the currently selected books to it, whenever a user submits the first form," explained Mike.

"Therefore, every form will send its data to the parent component and we will use the complete data for final submission, right?" Shawn asked.

"Exactly. We will need a way to store the incoming data in the parent component though."

```
// src/BookStore.js
// Updating BookStore component

var BookStore = React.createClass({
  getInitialState() {
    return ({ currentStep: 1, formValues: {} });
  },

  updateFormData(formData) {
```

```
      var formValues = Object.assign({}, this.state.formValues,
  formData);
      this.setState({formValues: formValues});
    },

    render() {
      switch (this.state.currentStep) {
        case 1:
          return <BookList updateFormData={this.updateFormData} />;
        case 2:
          return <ShippingDetails updateFormData={this.updateFormData}
  />;
        case 3:
          return <DeliveryDetails updateFormData={this.updateFormData}
  />;
      }
    }
  });
```

"We added state to store `formValues`. Whenever the user submits the form, the child form will call the parent's `updateFormData` function. This function will merge the current data stored in the parent's `formValues` with incoming `formData` and reset the state to the new `formValues`. In this case, we will get `selectedBooks` in the `formValues` object, as follows:" said Mike.

```
  { selectedBooks: ['Zero to One', 'Monk who sold his Ferrary'] }
```

"Note that, we are making use of another ES6 method—`Object.assign`. The `Object.assign()` method is used to copy the values of all the enumerable properties from one or more source objects to a target object."

"In our case, the use of `Object.assign` will merge the current state of form values with the new form values that are changed after some user interaction. We will then use this updated data to update the state of the component. We are using `Object.assign` instead of directly mutating the state of the component. We will cover why this is better than directly mutating the state of the component in the following chapters."

```
  var formValues = Object.assign({}, this.state.formValues, formData);
```

"Makes sense. This takes care of updating the form data. Now, how will we go to the next step?" Shawn asked.

"That's simple. Whenever we update the form data, we also need to update the `currentStep` method of the `BookStore` component. Can you give it a try?" Mike asked.

```js
// src/BookStore.js
// Updating BookStore component

var BookStore = React.createClass({
  updateFormData(formData) {
    var formValues = Object.assign({}, this.state.formValues,
formData);
    var nextStep = this.state.currentStep + 1;
    this.setState({currentStep: nextStep, formValues: formValues});
    console.log(formData);
  },

  render() {
    switch (this.state.currentStep) {
      case 1:
        return <BookList updateFormData={this.updateFormData} />;
      case 2:
        return <ShippingDetails updateFormData={this.updateFormData}
/>;
      case 3:
        return <DeliveryDetails updateFormData={this.updateFormData}
/>;
    }
  }
});
```

"Perfect. You have updated the step by 1 in the `updateFormData` callback. This will take the user to the next step." Mike.

Form validation

"Shawn, I think we should also add basic validation to the `BookList` component so that the user can't go to the next step without selecting a book," said Mike.

"Agree. Let me give it a try." answered Shawn.

```js
// src/BookStore.js
// Updating BookList component

var BookList = React.createClass({
```

```
getInitialState() {
  return (
    { books: [
      { id: 1, name: 'Zero to One', author: 'Peter Thiel' },
      { id: 2, name: 'Monk who sold his Fearrary', author: 'Robin
Sharma' },
      { id: 3, name: 'Wings of Fire', author: 'A.P.J. Abdul Kalam' }
    ],
      selectedBooks: [],
      error: false
    }
  );
},

_renderError() {
  if (this.state.error) {
    return (
      <div className="alert alert-danger">
        {this.state.error}
      </div>
    );
  }
},

handleSubmit(event) {
  event.preventDefault();

  if(this.state.selectedBooks.length === 0) {
    this.setState({error: 'Please choose at least one book to
continue'});
  } else {
    this.setState({error: false});
    this.props.updateFormData({ selectedBooks: this.state.
selectedBooks });
  }
},

render() {
  var errorMessage = this._renderError();

  return (
    <div>
      <h3> Choose from wide variety of books available in our store
</h3>
```

```
        {errorMessage}
        <form onSubmit={this.handleSubmit}>
            { this.state.books.map((book) => { return (this._
renderBook(book)); })}
            <input type="submit" className="btn btn-success" />
        </form>
    </div>
    );
    }
});
```

"I added the state to manage the validation error. Initially, it will be set to `false`. After the user submits the form, we will check whether the user has not selected anything and set an appropriate error message. State will be updated and it will display the error message accordingly. If the user has selected at least one book, then the error state will be set to `false` and the error message won't be displayed. We get a nice error message with some help from the Bootstrap classes." said Shawn.

Choose from wide variety of books available in our store

Please choose atleast one book to continue

☐ Zero to One -- Peter Thiel

☐ Monk who sold his Fearrary -- Robin Sharma

☐ Wings of Fire -- A.P.J. Abdul Kalam

[Submit]

"Awesome. Let's move to the second form now. We want to accept the user's shipping details such as the address and contact information." said Mike.

Shipping details step

"Shawn, in this step, we want to get the user's shipping preferences. It will contain the shipping address and name of the customer." explained Mike.

"We should also add a phone number." Shawn added.

"Sure thing. Here is how our shipping details form look like." informed Mike.

```
// src/BookStore.js
// Adding ShippingDetails component

var ShippingDetails = React.createClass({
  getInitialState() {
    return (
      { fullName: '', contactNumber: '', shippingAddress: '', error:
false }
    );
  },

  _renderError() {
    if (this.state.error) {
      return (
        <div className="alert alert-danger">
          {this.state.error}
        </div>
      );
    }
  },

  _validateInput() {
    if (this.state.fullName === '') {
      this.setState({error: "Please enter full name"});
    } else if (this.state.contactNumber === '') {
      this.setState({error: "Please enter contact number"});
    } else if (this.state.shippingAddress === '') {
      this.setState({error: "Please enter shipping address"});
    } else {
      this.setState({error: false});
      return true;
    }

  },

  handleSubmit(event) {
    event.preventDefault();

    var formData = { fullName: this.state.fullName,
                     contactNumber: this.state.contactNumber,
```

```
                    shippingAddress: this.state.shippingAddress };

    if (this._validateInput()) {
      this.props.updateFormData(formData);
    }
  },

  handleChange(event, attribute) {
    var newState = this.state;
    newState[attribute] = event.target.value;
    this.setState(newState);
    console.log(this.state);
  },

  render() {
    var errorMessage = this._renderError();

    return (
      <div>
        <h1>Enter your shipping information.</h1>
        {errorMessage}
        <div style={{width: 200}}>
          <form onSubmit={this.handleSubmit}>
            <div className="form-group">
              <input className="form-control"
                     type="text"
                     placeholder="Full Name"
                     value={this.state.fullName}
                     onChange={(event) => this.handleChange(event,
'fullName')} />
            </div>

            <div className="form-group">
              <input className="form-control"
                     type="text"
                     placeholder="Contact number"
                     value={this.state.contactNumber}
                     onChange={(event) => this.handleChange(event,
'contactNumber')}/>
            </div>

            <div className="form-group">
              <input className="form-control"
```

```
                    type="text"
                    placeholder="Shipping Address"
                    value={this.state.shippingAddress}
                    onChange={(event) => this.handleChange(event,
  'shippingAddress')} />
              </div>

          <div className="form-group">
            <button type="submit"
                    ref="submit"
                    className="btn btn-success">
              Submit
            </button>
          </div>
        </form>
      </div>
    </div>
  );
  }
});
```

"This component is using almost same code as our first form. We are showing textboxes for the shipping details to the user. There is validation and all the fields are required fields. We are syncing the data entered by the user using a `onChange` handler in the state of the component and passing this state to the `updateFormData` function of the parent component in the end." Mike explained.

"Now, at the end of second step, we have gathered a list of books chosen by the user and the shipping information." said Mike.

```
{ selectedBooks: ["Zero to One", "Wings of Fire"],
  fullName: "John Smith",
  contactNumber: "1234567890",
  shippingAddress: "10th Cross, NY" }
```

"I can see how we are assigning the `value` prop of the input fields to it's corresponding state." Shawn.

```
value={this.state.shippingAddress}
```

"Yes. As we discussed earlier about the controlled and uncontrolled components, we are making sure that the UI reflects the latest state, based on the user interaction." said Mike.

Delivery details step

"Shawn, the next step is about providing various delivery options. For now, let's assume that the user can choose between `Primary` delivery, meaning a next-day delivery, and `Normal` delivery, meaning 3 - 4 days delivery. By default, the `Primary` option must be selected. A user can choose the `Normal` delivery option too. Can you try building this last step?" Mike asked.

```
// src/BookStore.js
// Adding DeliveryDetails component

var DeliveryDetails = React.createClass({
  getInitialState() {
    return (
      { deliveryOption: 'Primary' }
    );
  },

  handleChange(event) {
    this.setState({ deliveryOption: event.target.value});
  },

  handleSubmit(event) {
    event.preventDefault();
    this.props.updateFormData(this.state);
  },

  render() {
    return (
      <div>
        <h1>Choose your delivery options here.</h1>
        <div style={{width:200}}>
          <form onSubmit={this.handleSubmit}>
            <div className="radio">
              <label>
                <input type="radio"
                       checked={this.state.deliveryOption ===
"Primary"}
                       value="Primary"
                       onChange={this.handleChange} />
                Primary -- Next day delivery
              </label>
            </div>
            <div className="radio">
```

```
                    <label>
                      <input type="radio"
                             checked={this.state.deliveryOption ===
      "Normal"}
                             value="Normal"
                             onChange={this.handleChange} />
                      Normal -- 3-4 days
                    </label>
                  </div>

                  <button className="btn btn-success">
                    Submit
                  </button>
                </form>
              </div>
            </div>
          );
        }
      });
```

"Mike, as needed, I added `Primary` as the default option through state. I used radio buttons and their checked prop in order to make sure that only one radio button is selected at any point of time. Also, the state is updated using the `onChange` callback to reflect the selected by option. Finally, the `updateFormData` function is called to update the parent's form data." Shawn explained.

"Great, Shawn. This looks good. I think we will also have to make some changes to our `BookStore` component as now we want to show a confirmation page after the user has completed choosing delivery options."

```
// src/BookStore.js
// Updating BookStore component

var BookStore = React.createClass({
  render() {
    switch (this.state.currentStep) {
      case 1:
        return <BookList updateFormData={this.updateFormData} />;
      case 2:
        return <ShippingDetails updateFormData={this.updateFormData}
/>;
      case 3:
        return <DeliveryDetails updateFormData={this.updateFormData}
/>;
      case 4:
```

```
            return <Confirmation data={this.state.formValues}/>;}/>;}/>;
         default:
            return <BookList updateFormData={this.updateFormData} />;
      }
   }
});

// Adding Conformation step

var Confirmation = React.createClass({
   render() {
      return (
         <div>
            <h1>Are you sure you want to submit the data?</h1>
         </div>
      );
   }
});
```

"We added the Confirmation component as the last step and also added the default form to be the BookList form, where the user can choose the books. Now, we just need to show all the information captured up to the last step on the **Confirmation** page and actually submit everything to the backend." said Mike.

"Let me update the **Confirmation** page to show the data entered by the user." Shawn said.

```
var Confirmation = React.createClass({
   handleSubmit(event) {
      event.preventDefault();
      this.props.updateFormData(this.props.data);
   },

   render() {
      return (
         <div>
            <h1>Are you sure you want to submit the data?</h1>
            <form onSubmit={this.handleSubmit}>
               <div>
                  <strong>Full Name</strong> : { this.props.data.fullName }
               </div><br/>
               <div>
                  <strong>Contact Number</strong> : { this.props.data.
contactNumber }
               </div><br/>
```

```
            <div>
               <strong>Shipping Address</strong> : { this.props.data.
   shippingAddress }
            </div><br/>
            <div>
               <strong>Selected books</strong> : { this.props.data.
   selectedBooks.join(", ") }
            </div><br/>
            <button className="btn btn-success">
               Place order
            </button>
         </form>
      </div>
    );
  }
});
```

"Mike, I listed all the data selected by the user and provided a button to place the order. It looks like this." Shawn.

Are you sure you want to submit the data?

Full Name : John Smith

Contact Number : 123456790

Shipping Address : Block 10, South St. NY

Selected books : Zero to One, Monk who sold his Fearrary

Place order

"Perfect. I have the success page ready. Let's try that." Mike.

```
// src/BookStore.js
// Adding Success step

var Success = React.createClass({
  render() {
    var numberOfDays = "1 to 2 ";

    if (this.props.data.deliveryOption === 'Normal') {
      numberOfDays = "3 to 4 ";
    }
```

```
      return (
        <div>
          <h2>
            Thank you for shopping with us {this.props.data.fullName}.
          </h2>
          <h4>
            You will soon get {this.props.data.selectedBooks.join(", ")}
at {this.props.data.shippingAddress} in arrorximately {numberOfDays}
days.
          </h4>
        </div>
      );
    }
});
```

"We will also need to update BookStore to show the success page," added Mike.

```
// Updating render method of BookStore component

  render() {
    switch (this.state.currentStep) {
      case 1:
        return <BookList updateFormData={this.updateFormData} />;
      case 2:
        return <ShippingDetails updateFormData={this.updateFormData}
/>;
      case 3:
        return <DeliveryDetails updateFormData={this.updateFormData}
/>;
      case 4:
        return <Confirmation data={this.state.formValues}
updateFormData={this.updateFormData}/>;
      case 5:
        return <Success data={this.state.formValues}/>;
      default:
        return <BookList updateFormData={this.updateFormData} />;
    }
  }
```

"Now, the success page will be shown as the last page after the user has confirmed and placed the order. Our first version of the form wizard is complete." Mike informed.

Thank you for shopping with us John Smith.

You will soon get Zero to One, Monk who sold his Fearrary at Block 10, South St. NY in approrximately 3 to 4 days.

Summary

In this chapter, we discussed how to develop forms in React. We saw how to use different input types and event handlers to respond to the user interaction for these inputs. We used state and props to manage the flow of form data from one step to another. We also saw how to use dynamic components to display particular form to the user based on the current step that the user is present on.

In the next chapter, we will continue with the form wizard and see how mixins can help us in organizing the code better.

5
Mixins and the DOM

In the previous chapter, we took a deep dive into React Forms. We took a look at building multiple components and interactivity between them, Controller and Uncontrolled Components, building Forms and Form elements, and Form events and handlers for the events. We build a form to capture cart-checkout flow and orders being placed in a multi-step form.

In this chapter, we will focus on abstracting content using mixins and touch upon DOM handling.

Here, we will cover the following points:

- Mixins
- PureRender mixin
- React and the DOM
- Refs

At the end of this chapter, we will be able to abstract and reuse logic across our components and learn how to handle DOM from within the components.

Back at the office

The duo was back at work. Mike entered with a cup of coffee. It was morning and the office had just started to buzz.

"So Shawn, we did a lot of complex forms stuff last time. Our cart flow is now complete. However, now we have been asked to add a timeout to the cart. We need to show a timer to the user that they need to checkout and complete the order in 15 minutes."

"Any idea how we can do this?"

"Umm, maintain a state for timer and keep updating every second? Take some action when the timer hits zero."

"Right! We will use intervals to reduce the timeout values and keep updating our views to display the timer. As we have been storing the form data in a single place, our `Bookstore` component, let's go ahead and add a state value that will track this timeout value. Let's change our initial state to something similar to the following:"

```
getInitialState() {
    return ({currentStep: 1, formValues: {}, cartTimeout: 60 * 15});
}
```

"60 X 15, that's 15 minutes in seconds value. We will also need to add a method to keep updating this state so that we can use it freely from here as well as the child components."

```
updateCartTimeout(timeout){
    this.setState({cartTimeout: timeout});
}
```

"Cool."

"Now, what we will do is define what are called as mixins."

"Mixins?"

"Yeah, mixins allow us to share a code across components. Let's take a look at how we are going to use it before moving ahead."

```
var SetIntervalMixin = {

  componentWillMount: function() {
    this.intervals = [];
  },

  setInterval: function() {
    this.intervals.push(setInterval.apply(null, arguments));
  },

  componentWillUnmount: function() {
    this.intervals.map(clearInterval);
  }
};

module.exports = SetIntervalMixin;
```

"So what we are doing here is nothing much but defining an object. We will see how we use it in our components."

"As you can see, what we are trying to achieve here is add a way to track all our interval handlers, as follows:"

```
componentWillMount: function() {
    this.intervals = [];
}
```

"Here, we are first initializing an array to hold instances to intervals that we will be creating. Next, we will define a method that can be used to define new intervals, as follows:"

```
setInterval: function() {
    this.intervals.push(setInterval.apply(null, arguments));
}
```

"Got it. I see the last bit is defining the `componentWillUnmount` method and we have already defined `componentWillMount`; but this isn't a React component. Why do we have these method here?"

"Oh right. Let's take a look at the following method first:"

```
componentWillUnmount: function() {
    this.intervals.map(clearInterval);
}
```

"What this method does is clean up the intervals, which we might have created, before we unmount our component."

"Got it."

"Now, as you mentioned, we have two life cycle methods here — `componentWillMount` and `componentWillUnmount`."

"When we start using this in our component, they are called just like the other similar methods, which we have in our component for life cycle."

"Oh nice. Will both this and the existing method get called?" Shawn asked.

"Exactly. Now that we have the mixing defined, let's start using it!"

"The first place we want to start using this is on the delivery details page. This is as simple as doing the following:"

```
var DeliveryDetails = React.createClass({
...
mixins: [SetIntervalMixin]
...
```

"Awesome, next we would like to start using this to take care of storing `cartTimout` values and updating them. Can you define a mixin to do just that?" asked Mike.

"Okay, I will first define a method to decrement the cart timer, something that will keep updating the state. Next, we will need to actually set the timeout, to call the method at an interval so that it is called every second to decrement the time?"

"Exactly, let's see how you would do it."

```
var CartTimeoutMixin = {
  componentWillMount: function () {
    this.setInterval(this.decrementCartTimer, 1000);
  },

  decrementCartTimer(){
    if (this.state.cartTimeout == 0) {
      this.props.alertCartTimeout();
      return;
    }
    this.setState({cartTimeout: this.state.cartTimeout - 1});
  },

};
```

"Nice, that's exactly what we need. But we missed one piece; we need to be able to send this back to that parent component to store back the timer value that we are updating here."

"We will also take care of passing the current state of timer from the parent to the children."

"Oh, right."

"Let's go back to our parent component to start passing the cart timer value to the children. Here's how our render method should look now:"

```
......
render() {
```

```
switch (this.state.currentStep) {

    case 1:
      return <BookList updateFormData={this.updateFormData}/>;

    case 2:
      return <ShippingDetails updateFormData={this.updateFormData}
                              cartTimeout={this.state.cartTimeout}
                              updateCartTimeout={this.
updateCartTimeout} />;

    case 3:
      return <DeliveryDetails updateFormData={this.updateFormData}
                              cartTimeout={this.state.cartTimeout}
                              updateCartTimeout={this.
updateCartTimeout} />;


    ......
```

"Notice that we are passing the `updateCartTimeout` method here. This is something that we will start using next in our mixin."

"Next, we are going to update the `DeliveryDetails` component to start storing the `cartTimeout` value."

```
getInitialState() {
    return { deliveryOption: 'Primary', cartTimeout: this.props.
cartTimeout };
  }
```

"With this setup, we can now set up our render method for the delivery options page, this should now look similar to the following:"

```
render() {

    var minutes = Math.floor(this.state.cartTimeout / 60);
    var seconds = this.state.cartTimeout - minutes * 60;

    return (
      <div>
        <h1>Choose your delivery options here.</h1>
        <div style={{width:200}}>
          <form onSubmit={this.handleSubmit}>
            <div className="radio">
```

```
            <label>

              <input type="radio"
                     checked={this.state.deliveryOption ===
  "Primary"}

                     value="Primary"
                     onChange={this.handleChange} />
              Primary -- Next day delivery
            </label>
          </div>

          <div className="radio">
            <label>
              <input type=e"radio"
                     checked={this.state.deliveryOption ===
  "Normal"}

                     value="Normal"
                     onChange={this.handleChange} />
              Normal -- 3-4 days
            </label>
          </div>

          <button className="btn btn-success">
            Submit
          </button>

        </form>
      </div>

      <div className="well">
          <span className="glyphicon glyphicon-time" aria-
  hidden="true"></span> You have {minutes} Minutes, {seconds} Seconds,
  before confirming order
          </div>

      </div>
    );
  }
```

"We also need to start using the `CartMixin`, so our `mixins` import should look
similar to the following:"

```
...
mixins: [SetIntervalMixin, CartTimeoutMixin],
...
```

"Nice, let me see how the shipping information looks like now."

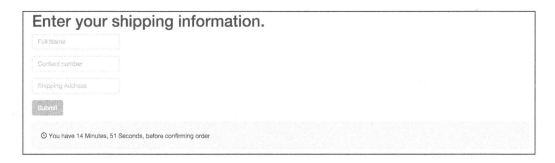

"It works!" exclaimed Shawn.

"Awesome. Remember, Shawn, now we need to pass the information back to our parent component when we change to some other page."

"Yeah, we should add it to the components, where we used the mixin?"

"Better yet, let's add the following code to the mixin:"

```
....
componentWillUnmount(){
    this.props.updateCartTimeout(this.state.cartTimeout);
  }
....
```

"Now our mixin should look similar to the following:"

```
var CartTimeoutMixin = {
  componentWillMount: function () {
    this.setInterval(this.decrementCartTimer, 1000);
  },

  decrementCartTimer(){
    if (this.state.cartTimeout == 0) {
      this.props.alertCartTimeout();
      return;
    }
    this.setState({cartTimeout: this.state.cartTimeout - 1});
  },

  componentWillUnmount(){
```

```
        this.props.updateCartTimeout(this.state.cartTimeout);
    }

};

    module.exports = CartTimeoutMixin;
```

"Our mixin will now update the current cart value when it gets unmounted."

"We missed one thing that is part of this mixin. We call `this.props.`
`alertCartTimeout()` when the timer hits zero."

"We are going to define this on the *parent component* and pass it around to be called
from child component, as follows:"

```
    alertCartTimeout(){
        this.setState({currentStep: 10});
    },
```

"Then update our render method to take care when we reach the timeout step, as
shown in the following:"

```
    render() {
        switch (this.state.currentStep) {
        case 1:
            return <BookList updateFormData={this.updateFormData}/>;
        case 2:
            return <ShippingDetails updateFormData={this.updateFormData}
                                    cartTimeout={this.state.cartTimeout}
                                    updateCartTimeout={this.
updateCartTimeout}
                                    alertCartTimeout={this.
alertCartTimeout}/>;
        case 3:
            return <DeliveryDetails updateFormData={this.updateFormData}
                                    cartTimeout={this.state.cartTimeout}
                                    updateCartTimeout={this.
updateCartTimeout}
                                    alertCartTimeout={this.
alertCartTimeout}/>;
        case 4:
            return <Confirmation data={this.state.formValues}
                                 updateFormData={this.updateFormData}
                                 cartTimeout={this.state.cartTimeout}/>;
        case 5:
```

```
      return <Success data={this.state.formValues}
cartTimeout={this.state.cartTimeout}/>;

    case 10:
      /* Handle the case of Cart timeout */
      return <div><h2>Your cart timed out, Please try again!</h2></
div>;
    default:
      return <BookList updateFormData={this.updateFormData}/>;
  }
}
```

Let's see how the `DeliveryDetails` component looks after completing it, now:"

```
import React from 'react';
import SetIntervalMixin from './mixins/set_interval_mixin'
import CartTimeoutMixin from './mixins/cart_timeout_mixin'

var DeliveryDetails = React.createClass({
  propTypes: {
    alertCartTimeout: React.PropTypes.func.isRequired,
    updateCartTimeout: React.PropTypes.func.isRequired,
    cartTimeout: React.PropTypes.number.isRequired
  },

  mixins: [SetIntervalMixin, CartTimeoutMixin],

  getInitialState() {
    return { deliveryOption: 'Primary', cartTimeout: this.props.
cartTimeout };
  },

  componentWillReceiveProps(newProps){
    this.setState({cartTimeout: newProps.cartTimeout});
  },


  handleChange(event) {
    this.setState({ deliveryOption: event.target.value});
  },

  handleSubmit(event) {
    event.preventDefault();
    this.props.updateFormData(this.state);
  },

  render() {
```

```
      var minutes = Math.floor(this.state.cartTimeout / 60);
      var seconds = this.state.cartTimeout - minutes * 60;
      return (
        <div>
          <h1>Choose your delivery options here.</h1>
          <div style={{width:200}}>
            <form onSubmit={this.handleSubmit}>
              <div className="radio">
                <label>
                  <input type="radio"
                         checked={this.state.deliveryOption ===
"Primary"}
                         value="Primary"
                         onChange={this.handleChange} />
                  Primary -- Next day delivery
                </label>
              </div>
              <div className="radio">
                <label>
                  <input type="radio"
                         checked={this.state.deliveryOption ===
"Normal"}
                         value="Normal"
                         onChange={this.handleChange} />
                  Normal -- 3-4 days
                </label>
              </div>

              <button className="btn btn-success">
                Submit
              </button>
            </form>
          </div>
          <div className='well'>
            <span className="glyphicon glyphicon-time" aria-
hidden="true"></span> You have {minutes} Minutes, {seconds} Seconds,
before confirming order
          </div>
        </div>
      );
    }
});

module.exports = DeliveryDetails;
```

"We are also going to update our `ShippingDetails` component to look similar to the following:"

```
import React from 'react';

import SetIntervalMixin from './mixins/set_interval_mixine'
import CartTimeoutMixin from './mixins/cart_timeout_mixin'



var ShippingDetails = React.createClass({
  propTypes: {
    alertCartTimeout:React.PropTypes.func.isRequired,
    updateCartTimeout: React.PropTypes.func.isRequired,
    cartTimeout: React.PropTypes.number.isRequired
  },

  mixins: [SetIntervalMixin, CartTimeoutMixin],

  getInitialState() {
    return {fullName: '', contactNumber: '', shippingAddress: '',
error: false, cartTimeout: this.props.cartTimeout};
  },
  _renderError() {
    if (this.state.error) {
      return (
        <div className=e"alert alert-danger">
          {this.state.error}
        </div>
      );
    }
  },

  _validateInput() {
    …..
  },

  handleSubmit(event) {
    ….
  },

  handleChange(event, attribute) {
    var newState = this.state;
    newState[attribute] = event.target.value;
```

```
      this.setState(newState);
      console.log(this.state);
    },

  render() {
    var errorMessage = this._renderError();
    var minutes = Math.floor(this.state.cartTimeout / 60);
    var seconds = this.state.cartTimeout - minutes * 60;

    return (
      <div>
        <h1>Enter your shipping information.</h1>
          ....


        <div className='well'>
            <span className="glyphicon glyphicon-time" aria-
hidden="true"></span> You have {minutes} Minutes, {seconds} Seconds,
before confirming order
        </div>
      </div>
    );
  }
});

module.exports = ShippingDetails;
```

It should start looking similar to the following screenshot now:

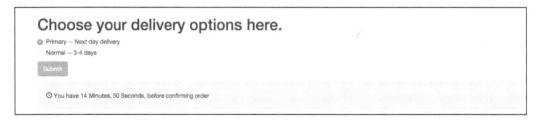

"Awesome," exclaimed Shawn.

"In case of timeouts, we have a simple display:"

> Your cart timed out, Please try again!

Adding a modal

"Alright, this works well," continued Mike.

"However, it's a bit clumsy right now. After the timeout, there's nothing a user can do. We can add a popup to notify the user. Instead of showing the error page, let's display a modal with an alert and redirect the user to the first page so that the user can restart the flow. We can use Bootstrap modal to achieve this."

"Got it. Want me to give it a try?" asked Shawn.

"Go ahead!"

"Let me start with setting up the modal first. I will use a simple bootstrap modal to display it. After that's done, I will need to invoke display of the modal from `alertCartTimeout`, I guess. I will also be setting up to display the first page and reset form data."

"Correct."

"This is how the modal will look"

```
import React from 'react';

var ModalAlertTimeout = React.createClass({
  render() {
    return (

      <div className="modal fade" ref='timeoutModal'>
        <div className="modal-dialog">
          <div className="modal-content">
            <div className="modal-header">
              <button type="button" className="close" data-
dismiss="modal" aria-label="Close"><span aria-hidden="true">x</span></
button>
              <h4 className="modal-title">Timeout</h4>
            </div>
```

```
                    <div className="modal-body">
                      <p>The cart has timed-out. Please try again!</p>
                    </div>
                  </div>
                </div>
              </div>
            );
        }
    });
    module.exports = ModalAlertTimeout;
```

"Nice. Next, you will be updating the `Bookstore` component `alertCartTimeout` method."

"Yeah, I added a new empty HTML element with the `modalAlertTimeout` ID to the body. This will be used to display new modal and mount component on top of it. I also changed alert timeout method to the following:"

```
alertCartTimeout(){
    React.render(<ModalAlertTimeout />, document.getElementById('modal
AlertTimeout'));
    this.setState({currentStep: 1, formValues: {}, cartTimeout: 1});
}
```

"Ah, let's see what this does" continued Mike, checking the changes that Shawn had done."

"Shawn, looks like the timeout is taking us to the first page, but its not displaying the modal alert"

"Oh, right. We still need to invoke the display of the modal from bootstrap."

"Correct. Let me take care of that, Shawn. In our `ModalAlertTimeout`, we will add a method call to display the modal after the component has successfully mounted, as follows:"

```
componentDidMount(){
    setTimeout(()=> {
      let timeoutModal = this.refs.timeoutModal.getDOMNode();
      $(timeoutModal).modal('show');
    }, 100);
}
```

"Ah, I see we are doing some DOM stuff here."

"Yeah, let me go over them."

Refs

"I think we have used this before," asked Shawn.

"Yeah. What refs do is give us a handle to refer to some part of the component. We have done this in forms. Here, we are using it to get a handle to the modal so that we can invoke the `modal()` method on top of it."

"This would, in turn, display the modal."

"Now, notice how we are using the `getDOMNode()` method."

"Yup. What does it do?"

"The `getDOMNode()` method helps us to get the underlying DOM node, where the React element is rendered. In our case, we want to invoke a method on the DOM node."

"When we call `this.refs.timeoutModal`, it returns us a ref object of the component."

"This is different from the actual DOM component. It's actually a React-wrapped object. To grab the underlying DOM object, we invoked `getDOMNode()`."

"Got it."

"Next, we have wrapped all this in a `setTimeout` call so that we can call it after the React component is successfully rendered and modal content exists on the page."

"Finally, we called `$(timeoutModal).modal('show')` to invoke the modal!"

"Let's see how our modal looks now."

```
import React from 'react';

var ModalAlertTimeout = React.createClass({
  componentDidMount() {
    setTimeout(() => {
      let timeoutModal = this.refs.timeoutModal.getDOMNode();
      $(timeoutModal).modal('show');
    }, 100);
  },

  render() {
    return (

      <div className="modal fade" ref='timeoutModal'>
```

```
        <div className="modal-dialog">
          <div className="modal-content">
            <div className="modal-header">
              <button type="button" className="close" data-
    dismiss="modal" aria-label="Close"><span aria-hidden="true">×</span></
    button>
              <h4 className="modal-title">Timeout</h4>
            </div>
            <div className="modal-body">
              <p>The cart has timed-out. Please try again!</p>
            </div>
          </div>
        </div>
      );
    }
  });
  module.exports = ModalAlertTimeout;
```

"Let's see how this looks now."

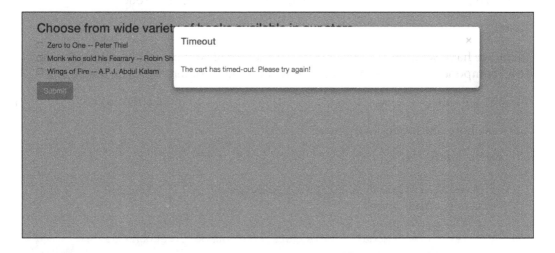

"One last thing since we are discussing this, is about DOM. We can invoke `getDOMNode()` to also get the node for the current component. Therefore, we can simply call `this.getDOMNode()` and that will also return us an element!"

"Alright, let's do this. We will unmount the modal when someone closes it so that we can invoke it afresh on the second render."

"Let's define a callback method to do just that, as follows:"

```
unMountComponent () {
    React.unmountComponentAtNode(this.getDOMNode().parentNode);
}
```

"Finally, we will set this as a callback on close of our modal, as follows:"

```
$(timeoutModal).on('hidden.bs.modal', this.unMountComponent);
```

"With this, we are done! The component will unmount on modal hide."

"Notice how we are using the `parentNode` attribute on the DOM node to hide the modal. This helps us to get the container on which the React element is and that we are using to remove the modal."

"Nice. That has been a refresher. Thanks Mike!"

With that, the duo headed back to check the various changes they had just done.

Summary

In this chapter, we took a look at refactoring our components. We saw how to make use of mixins and extract similar functionalities to use seamlessly across components. We also took a look at DOM interactions, using refs, and related DOM actions from a component.

In the next chapter, we will explore how React functions on the the server side. We will see how React allows us to render and handle components on the server to pre-render HTML, which is useful for several reasons. We will also take a look at how this affects the React component life cycle.

6

React on the Server

In the previous chapter, we took a look at refactoring our components. We saw how to make use of mixins and extract similar functionalities to use seamlessly across components. We also took a look at DOM interactions, using refs, and related DOM actions from a component.

In this chapter, we will explore how React functions on the server side. React allows us to render and handle components on the server to pre-render HTML, which is useful for several reasons. We will also take a look at how this affects the React component life cycle.

In this chapter, we will cover the following points:

- Server-side rendering
- Render functions
- Server-side component life cycle

At the end of chapter, we will be able to start using React components on the server side and understand its interactions and implications with the server side.

Getting React to render on server

"Hey Shawn!" Mike startled Shawn, entering their workplace with a cup of coffee.

"Good morning, Mike," replied Shawn.

Sun sparkled on Shawn's desk and they entered into a conversation about a new project that they were about to begin.

"Shawn, I just came to know, from Carla, about a new project that we need to take. The client has asked us to build a simple search page for our Open Library project."

Shawn and Mike had previously build an application to display recent changes from `openlibrary.com` API. They were now going to build a search application on top of Open Library's Search API.

"Awesome," Mike was excited about this. He was already loving working on React.

"Shawn, for this project, we will be exploring options on how to use React on the server."

Until now, we have been manually mounting our components after page load. Until the component is rendered, the page doesn't have any HTML content from the component.

"Let's see how we will be doing this on the server so that HTML is pre-generated on the page instead of after the page has completely loaded."

"Got it. How is rendering of components on server side useful though?"

"It is useful for a couple of reasons. One being that we are generating content on the server. This is useful for SEO purpose and better indexing with search engines."

"As the content is generated on the server, the first render would display the page immediately instead of waiting for the page load to properly finish, after which the component would be rendered."

"This also helps us to avoid a flicker effect on our page loads. There are other such niceties that we can harness, we'll explore them later," Mike explained.

"Cool. Let's begin then."

"Alright! For this project, let's begin with a starter Webpack Project to manage our code. For the server element, we will be using Express JS. We won't be doing anything complex here, we will simply expose a route from Express JS and render a `.ejs` view that consists of our component."

"An example of such a starter project can be found on the `http://webpack.github.io/` website," informed Mike.

"Cool, I think we will divide the code on client/server side as well?"

"Yes. Let's put them under the `/app` directory to consist our components, `/client` for client-specific code, and `/server` for the code to be used on server in our `/src` directory," continued Mike.

"Next, we will be setting up the `server.js` file in `/app/server` directory."

```
import path from 'path';
import Express from 'express';

var app = Express();
var server;

const PATH_STYLES = path.resolve(__dirname, '../client/styles');
const PATH_DIST = path.resolve(__dirname, '../../dist');

app.use('/styles', Express.static(PATH_STYLES));
app.use(Express.static(PATH_DIST));

app.get('/', (req, res) => {
  res.sendFile(path.resolve(__dirname, '../client/index.html'));
});

server = app.listen(process.env.PORT || 3000, () => {
  var port = server.address().port;

  console.log('Server is listening at %s', port);
});
```

"That's a pretty standard Express App setup. We are specifying the styles to be used, static assets path, and so on."

"For our route, we are simple exposing the root / by doing this:"

```
app.get('/', (req, res) => {
  res.sendFile(path.resolve(__dirname, '../client/index.html'));
});
```

"We are asking Express to serve the `index.html` file on request to root. In our `index.js` file, which we will be passing to node to run the application, we will simply expose the server module that we just wrote."

```
require('babel/register');

module.exports = require('./server');
```

"Mike, why do we require babel/register here?"

"Oh right. Here, we require Babel (`http://babeljs.io/`) to convert our files to browser-compatible format. We are using some JavaScript ES2015 syntax goodness. Babel helps us to add support for the latest version of JavaScript through syntax transformers. This allows us to use the latest JavaScript syntax, which is not supported by browsers right now."

"With this setup, we will define our `index.html` as:"

```
<!DOCTYPE html>
<html>
<head lang="en">
  <meta charset="UTF-8">
  <title>Search</title>

  <link href="styles/main.css" rel="stylesheet" />

  <link rel="stylesheet" href="//maxcdn.bootstrapcdn.com/
bootstrap/3.3.5/css/bootstrap.min.css">
  <link rel="stylesheet" href="//maxcdn.bootstrapcdn.com/
bootstrap/3.3.5/css/bootstrap-theme.min.css">
<link rel="stylesheet" href="//maxcdn.bootstrapcdn.com/font-
awesome/4.4.0/css/font-awesome.min.css">

</head>
<body>
  <div id="app"></div>
  <script src="bundle.js"></script>
</body>
</html>
```

"Nothing much is going on over here. We are simply defining a single div on top of which we will be rendering the React component."

"Also, notice that we have included links to the files to add Bootstrap and Font Awesome support to our app."

"Next, on the client-side render handling, we would be doing"

```
// file: scr/client/scripts/client.js
import App from '../../app';

var attachElement = document.getElementById('app');
var state = {};
var app;

// Create new app and attach to element
```

```
app = new App({ state: state});

app.renderToDOM(attachElement);
```

"Finally, let's see how the `App` class defined here is used before moving to our actual component."

```
import React from 'react/addons';
import AppRoot from './components/AppRoot';

class App {
  constructor(options) {
    this.state = options.state;
  }

  render(element) {
    var appRootElement = React.createElement(AppRoot, {
      state: this.state
    });

    // render to DOM
    if (element) {
      React.render(appRootElement, element);
      return;
    }

    // render to string
    return React.renderToString(appRootElement);
  }

  renderToDOM(element) {
    if (!element) {
      new Error('App.renderToDOM: element is required');
    }

    this.render(element);
  }

  renderToString() {
    return this.render();
  }
}

export default App;
```

"Wow, that's a lot to sink in," exhaled Shawn.

"Hah! Give it some time. What we are doing here is simply taking care of our rendering logic. If we pass an element to this class, contents are rendered onto it; otherwise, we will return the rendered string version. Notice how we are using `React.renderToString` to achieve the same. Let's complete this first and we will then revisit it when we will be using it to render the contents on the server request."

"In a nutshell, we are just asking React to take in a state for a component, render it, and return the contents that would be rendered from the `render()` method as a string."

"We will then start by defining our root container component."

```
require("jquery");
import React from 'react/addons';
import SearchPage from './SearchPage'

var AppRoot = React.createClass({
    propTypes: {
      state: React.PropTypes.object.isRequired
    },
    render()
    {
      return <SearchPage/>;
    }
  })
  ;

export default AppRoot;
```

"Here, we simply define a container to hold our main component and require all our dependencies. Let's start building our Search Component next."

"Awesome. I think I can take that up. Looks like this will just be a simple component?"

"Yup. Go ahead," replied Mike.

"Ok, I see that we would be needing to fetch data from the Open Library API endpoint."

```
https://openlibrary.org/search.json?page=1&q=searchTerm
```

"Here the q query parameter will be the search term. An example response looks like:"

```
{
  "start": 0,
  "num_found": 6,
  "numFound": 6,
  "docs": [
    {
      "title_suggest": "Automatic search term variant generation for
document retrieval",
      "edition_key": [
        ..
      ],
  ...
      ],
      "author_name": [
  ..
  ..}]
}
```

"Right," added Mike.

"I think I will start by defining the initial status based on the start, num_found, and docs fields," said Shawn

"Okay."

```
getInitialState(){
    return {docs: [], numFound: 0, num_found: 0, start: 0,
searchCompleted: false, searching: false}
    }
```

"I also added two other states that I will maintain: searchCompleted to know whether the current search operation has completed or not and searching to know that we are currently searching something."

"Cool. Let's see the render method next," continued Mike.

"Let me start by adding the search box in the render method."

```
render() {
    let tabStyles = {paddingTop: '5%'};
    return (
        <div className='container'>
          <div className="row" style={tabStyles}>
            <div className="col-lg-8 col-lg-offset-2">
              <div className="input-group">
```

```
                    <input type="text" className="form-control"
        placeholder="Search for Projects..." ref='searchInput'/>
                 <span className="input-group-btn">
                    <button className="btn btn-default" type="button"
        onClick={this.performSearch}>Go!</button>
                 </span>
               </div>
             </div>
           </div>
         </div>
      );
    },
```

"We should now have a display for the search box."

Lord of the Rings			Go!
Total Results: 468			
Title	**Title suggest**	**Author**	**Edition**
The Lord of the Rings	The Lord of the Rings	J. R. R. Tolkien	120
The Lord of The Rings	The Lord of The Rings	J. R. R. Tolkien	47
Lord of the Rings	Lord of the Rings	Cedco Publishing	5
The Lord of The Rings	The Lord of The Rings	J. R. R. Tolkien	45
The Lord of The Rings	The Lord of The Rings	J. R. R. Tolkien	36
Lords of the Ring	Lords of the Ring	Doug Moe	2
Lord of the Rings	Lord of the Rings	Ernest Mathijs	2
Lord of the Rings	Lord of the Rings	Steven A. Schwartz	1
Lord of the rings	Lord of the rings		1
Lords of the Ring	Lords of the Ring		1
Lords of the Ring	Lords of the Ring	Peter Arnold	1
Lord of the Rings	Lord of the Rings	Reiner Knizia	1
Lord of the Rings	Lord of the Rings	J. R. R. Tolkien	1

"Next, we will add the `performSearch` method that initiates searching based on the search term entered by the user."

```
performSearch(){
  let searchTerm = $(this.refs.searchInput.getDOMNode()).val();
  this.openLibrarySearch(searchTerm);
  this.setState({searchCompleted: false, searching: true});
},
```

"Here, we are simply fetching the search term entered by the user and passing it to the `openLibrarySearch` method, which will actually perform the search. Then, we update the state that we are actively performing a search now."

"Let's complete the search functionality now."

```
openLibrarySearch(searchTerm){
  let openlibraryURI = `https://openlibrary.org/search.
json?page=1&q=${searchTerm}}`;
  fetch(openlibraryURI)
      .then(this.parseJSON)
      .then(this.updateState)
      .catch(function (ex) {
        console.log('Parsing failed', ex)
      })
}
```

"Ah, nice Shawn, you are using `fetch` instead of regular Ajax!"

"Huh, yeah. I have been using `https://github.com/github/fetch` as a polyfill for the `window.fetch` specification."

"Nice, isn't it? It supports simple and clean API, such as Ajax, and a unified fetching API."

After fetching of some resource or request completion, the callbacks fall through this are defined by the `then` method. Notice that we have also used ES2015 string literal to build the URI," added Shawn.

"Cool. Looks like you are fetching the resource, then passing it to `parseJSON` to parse and return the JSON result from the response body. Then, are we updating the state on top of it?"

"Yes, let me define those"

```
parseJSON(response) {
  return response.json();
},

// response.json() is returning the JSON content from the response.

updateState(json){
  this.setState({
    ...json,
    searchCompleted: true,
    searching: false
  });
},
```

"After getting the final response, I am updating and setting the state to result that is returned as well as updating our searchCompleted and searching states to indicate the searching job is done."

"Ah, nice Shawn, I see that you have started adopting and using new features from JS Next!, like the spread operator."

"Haha, yeah. I've fallen in love with these. I am using this to merge the properties of the JSON result with the new keys that I want to add and build a new object. This would also be done similarly using Object.assign that we previously saw."

```
Object.assign({}, json, {searchCompleted: true, searching: false} )
```

"That way, we are building a new object instead of mutating a previous one."

"Nice Shawn," Mike was happy knowing that Shawn was getting hang of the new things.

"Finally, let me add the loading action display to show a loader icon and display of actual results. The render method will now look like this."

```
render() {
  let tabStyles = {paddingTop: '5%'};
  return (
    <div className='container'>
      <div className="row" style={tabStyles}>
```

```
        <div className="col-lg-8 col-lg-offset-2">
          <div className="input-group">
            <input type="text" className="form-control"
placeholder="Search for Projects..." ref='searchInput'/>
            <span className="input-group-btn">
              <button className="btn btn-default" type="button"
onClick={this.performSearch}>Go!</button>
            </span>
          </div>
        </div>
      </div>
      { (() => {
        if (this.state.searching) {
          return this.renderSearching();
        }
        return this.state.searchCompleted ? this.
renderSearchElements() : <div/>
      })() }
    </div>
  );
},
```

"Here, we are checking the current state of the search operation. Based on this, we are displaying the loader of the actual contents, results, or empty div element."

"Let me define the loading and rendering of the elements."

```
renderSearching(){
    return <div className="row">
      <div className="col-lg-8 col-lg-offset-2">
        <div className='text-center'><i className="fa fa-spinner fa-
pulse fa-5x"></i></div>
      </div>
    </div>;
},
```

"This will define the display of the spinner to indicate loading."

```
renderSearchElements(){
    return (

        <div className="row">
          <div className="col-lg-8 col-lg-offset-2">
```

```
        <span className='text-center'>Total Results: {this.state.
numFound}</span>

          <table className="table table-stripped">
            <thead>
            <th>Title</th>
            <th>Title suggest</th>
            <th>Author</th>
            <th>Edition</th>
            </thead>
            <tbody>
            {this.renderDocs(this.state.docs)}
            </tbody>
          </table>

        </div>
      </div>

    );
  },

  renderDocs(docs){
    return docs.map((doc) => {
      console.log(doc);
      return <tr key={doc.cover_edition_key}>
        <td>{doc.title}</td>
        <td>{doc.title_suggest}</td>
        <td>{(doc.author_name || []).join(', ')}</td>
        <td>{doc.edition_count}</td>
      </tr>
    })
  },
```

"After adding this, the searching operation should display a loader like so."

The results displayed would look like this:

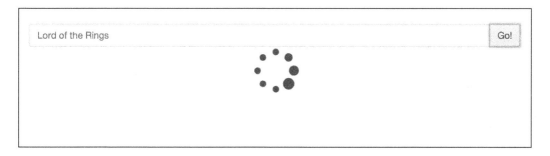

"The completed `SearchPage` component is as follows:"

```
import React from 'react';
var SearchPage = React.createClass({
  getInitialState(){
    return {docs: [], numFound: 0, num_found: 0, start: 0,
searchCompleted: false, searching: false}
  },
  render() {
    let tabStyles = {paddingTop: '5%'};
    return (
      <div className='container'>
        <div className="row" style={tabStyles}>
          <div className="col-lg-8 col-lg-offset-2">
            <div className="input-group">
              <input type="text" className="form-control"
placeholder="Search for Projects..." ref='searchInput'/>
              <span className="input-group-btn">
                <button className="btn btn-default" type="button"
onClick={this.performSearch}>Go!</button>
              </span>
            </div>
          </div>
        </div>
        { (() => {
          if (this.state.searching) {
            return this.renderSearching();
          }
          return this.state.searchCompleted ? this.
renderSearchElements() : <div/>
        })()}
      </div>
```

```
        );
      },
    renderSearching(){
      return <div className="row">
        <div className="col-lg-8 col-lg-offset-2">
          <div className='text-center'><i className="fa fa-spinner fa-
pulse fa-5x"></i></div>
        </div>
      </div>;
    },
    renderSearchElements(){
      return (
        <div className="row">
          <div className="col-lg-8 col-lg-offset-2">
            <span className='text-center'>Total Results: {this.state.
numFound}</span>
            <table className="table table-stripped">
              <thead>
              <th>Title</th>
              <th>Title suggest</th>
              <th>Author</th>
              <th>Edition</th>
              </thead>
              <tbody>
              {this.renderDocs(this.state.docs)}
              </tbody>
            </table>
          </div>
        </div>
      );
    },
    renderDocs(docs){
      return docs.map((doc) => {
        console.log(doc);
        return <tr key={doc.cover_edition_key}>
          <td>{doc.title}</td>
          <td>{doc.title_suggest}</td>
          <td>{(doc.author_name || []).join(', ')}</td>
          <td>{doc.edition_count}</td>
        </tr>
      })
    },

    performSearch(){
```

```
      let searchTerm = $(this.refs.searchInput.getDOMNode()).val();
      this.openLibrarySearch(searchTerm);
      this.setState({searchCompleted: false, searching: true});
    },

    parseJSON(response) {    return response.json();    },

    updateState(json) {
      this.setState({
        ...json,
        searchCompleted: true,
        searching: false
      });
    },
    openLibrarySearch(searchTerm) {
      let openlibraryURI = `https://openlibrary.org/search.
json?page=1&q=${searchTerm}}`;
      fetch(openlibraryURI)
        .then(this.parseJSON)
        .then(this.updateState)
        .catch(function (ex) {
          console.log('Parsing failed', ex)
        })
    }
});
module.exports = SearchPage;
```

"If you notice, I have used an immediately-invoked function to add an `if` statement to display the search icon rendering, as follows:"

```
        { (() => {
          if (this.state.searching) {
            return this.renderSearching();
          }
          return this.state.searchCompleted ? this.
renderSearchElements() : <div/>
            })()}
```

"Here, we have used the `() =>{}` syntax to define the function first and then immediately invoke it `(() =>{}))()`, returning the content that we need to display during the render."

"Great work, Shawn!" Mike was happy with the progress Shawn had made.

"This is handy, when we want to add simple logic switches within the render itself, instead of defining new methods," continued Mike.

On the server

"Now Shawn, let's pre-render the component on the server. What this means is that create an HTML element out of the React component and render its contents in our view on first page load itself. Currently, the loading of the element is taken care of by the client-side code."

```
app.renderToDOM(attachElement);
```

"Instead of this, we will render the React element in the Express action itself."

"First, let's set up an `.ejs` view to display out HTML contents along with dynamically-generated React contents."

```html
<!DOCTYPE html>
<html>
<head lang="en">
  <meta charset="UTF-8">
  <title>Search</title>

  <link href="styles/main.css" rel="stylesheet" />
  <link rel="stylesheet" href="https://maxcdn.bootstrapcdn.com/
bootstrap/3.3.5/css/bootstrap.min.css">
  <link rel="stylesheet" href="https://maxcdn.bootstrapcdn.com/
bootstrap/3.3.5/css/bootstrap-theme.min.css">
  <link rel="stylesheet" href="https://maxcdn.bootstrapcdn.com/font-
awesome/4.4.0/css/font-awesome.min.css">
</head>
<body>
  <div id="app">
  <%- reactOutput %>
  </div>
  <script src="bundle.js"></script>
</body>
</html>
```

"Here, we will pass `reactOutput` to the view as a variable to be rendered."

"We will now change our `server.js` file to include the required component and React for rendering."

```js
import AppRoot from '../app/components/AppRoot'
import React from 'react/addons';
```

"Our action will get changed to:"

```
app.get('/', (req, res) => {
  var reactAppContent = React.renderToString(<AppRoot state={{} }/>);
  console.log(reactAppContent);
  res.render(path.resolve(__dirname, '../client/index.ejs'),
{reactOutput: reactAppContent});
});
```

"Our final server code would look like."

```
import path from 'path';
import Express from 'express';

import AppRoot from '../app/components/AppRoot'
import React from 'react/addons';

var app = Express();
var server;

const PATH_STYLES = path.resolve(__dirname, '../client/styles');
const PATH_DIST = path.resolve(__dirname, '../../dist');

app.use('/styles', Express.static(PATH_STYLES));
app.use(Express.static(PATH_DIST));

app.get('/', (req, res) => {
  var reactAppContent = React.renderToString(<AppRoot state={{} }/>);
  console.log(reactAppContent);
  res.render(path.resolve(__dirname, '../client/index.ejs'),
{reactOutput: reactAppContent});
});

server = app.listen(process.env.PORT || 3000, () => {
  var port = server.address().port;

  console.log('Server is listening at %s', port);
});
```

"Here you have it! We are using React's `renderToString` method to render a component, passing any state if required, to accompany it."

Summary

In this chapter, we took a look at how server-side rendering can be used with React with the help of Express.js. We started with a client-side React component and in the end, replaced it with server-side rendering using the methods provided by the React API.

In the next chapter, we will look at React add ons for doing two-way binding, class name manipulation, cloning components, immutability helpers, and PureRenderMixin, while continuing with the search project build in this chapter.

7
React Addons

In the previous chapter, we learned to use React on the server side. We understood pre-rendering of the React components and changes in the component life cycle when using React on server. We also saw how to use server-side API of React using Express.js.

In this chapter, we will look at React addons—utility packages that are not a part of React core, however, they make development process fun and enjoyable. We will learn to use immutability helpers, cloning of components, and test utilities in this chapter. We will not be covering other addons such as `Animation`, `Perf`, and `PureRenderMixin`. These addons will be covered in the following chapters.

In this chapter, we will cover the following topics:

- Getting started with React addons
- Immutability helpers
- Cloning React components
- Test helpers

Getting started with Addons

After completing the previous project about using React on server side, Mike's team got some free time before starting the next project. Mike decided to utilize this time by learning about React addons.

"Shawn, we got some free time. Let's use it to get started with React addons."

"What are React addons? Are they related to React core library?" Shawn asked.

"React addons are utility modules that are not a part of the React core library. However, they are blessed by the React team. In future, some of them might be included in the React core. These libraries provide helpers for writing immutable code, utilities for testing React apps, and ways to measure and improve the performance of React apps." explained Mike.

"Each addon has its own npm package, making it to simple to use. For example, to use the Update addon, we need to install and require its npm package."

```
$ npm install  react-addons-update --save
```

```
// src/App.js
import Update from 'react-addons-update';
```

Immutability helpers

"Shawn, as we are learning about addons, let's add the sorting feature to our app so that the users can sort the books by their titles. I have already added the required markup for it."

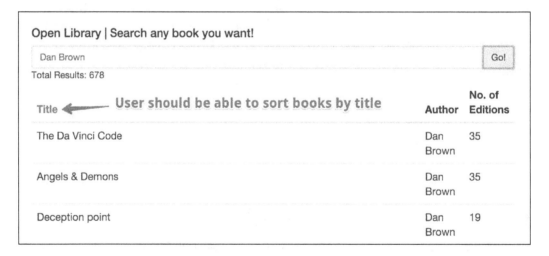

"Can you try writing the code for sorting when a user clicks on the **Title** heading?" Mark asked.

"Here it is. I introduced the sorting state to indicate the direction of sorting — ascending or descending."

```
// Updated getInitialState function of App component
// src/App.js

getInitialState(){
  return { books: [],
           totalBooks: 0,
           searchCompleted: false,
           searching: false,
           sorting: 'asc' };
}
```

"When the user clicks on **Title**, it will sort the books stored in the existing state in ascending or descending order using the sort-by npm package and update the state with the sorted books."

```
import sortBy from 'sort-by';

_sortByTitle() {
    let sortByAttribute = this.state.sorting === 'asc' ? "title" :
"-title";
    let unsortedBooks = this.state.books;
    let sortedBooks = unsortedBooks.sort(sortBy(sortByAttribute));
    this.setState({ books: sortedBooks,
                sorting: this._toggleSorting() });
},

_toggleSorting() {
   return this.state.sorting === 'asc' ? 'desc' : 'asc';
}
```

"Shawn, this is functional; however, it's not following the React way. React assumes that the state object is immutable. Here we are using reference to the books from the existing state when we are assigning value to `unsortedBooks`."

```
let unsortedBooks = this.state.books;
```

"Later, we are mutating `unsortedBooks` into `sortedBooks`; however, as a side-effect, we are also mutating the current value of `this.state`."

```
_sortByTitle() {
    let sortByAttribute = this.state.sorting === 'asc' ? "title" :
"-title";
```

```
    let unsortedBooks = this.state.books;
    console.log("Before sorting :");
    console.log(this.state.books[0].title);
    let sortedBooks = unsortedBooks.sort(sortBy(sortByAttribute));
    console.log("After sorting :");
    console.log(this.state.books[0].title);
    // this.setState({ books: sortedBooks,
                    sorting: this._toggleSorting() });

},
```

```
Before sorting :
187 men to avoid
After sorting :
Ḥaqīqat al-khadī'ah =
```

"As you can see, even if we commented call to this.setState, our current state is still mutated." Mark explained.

"This can be easily fixed using Object.assign from ES6. We can simply create a new array and copy the current value of this.state.books in it. We can then sort the new array and call setState with the new sorted array." informed Shawn.

 The Object.assign method copies the values of all the enumerable properties from multiple source objects in a target. More details can be found at the following: https://developer.mozilla.org/en/docs/Web/JavaScript/Reference/Global_Objects/Object/assign.

```
_sortByTitle() {
    let sortByAttribute = this.state.sorting === 'asc' ? "title" :
"-title";
    let unsortedBooks = Object.assign([], this.state.books);
    console.log("Before sorting :");
    console.log(this.state.books[0].title);
    let sortedBooks = unsortedBooks.sort(sortBy(sortByAttribute));
    console.log("After sorting :");
    console.log(this.state.books[0].title);
    this.setState({ books: sortedBooks,
                sorting: this._toggleSorting() });
}
```

```
Before sorting :
Ḥaqīqat al-khadi‘ah =
After sorting :
Ḥaqīqat al-khadi‘ah =
```

"Yes. This works. But the `Object.assign` method will make a shallow copy of `this.state.books`. It will create a new `unsortedBooks` object, however, it will still use the same references from `this.state.books` in `unsortedBooks`. Let's say, for some reason, we want the titles of all books in uppercase letters, then we may accidently mutate `this.state` too," Mike explained.

```
_sortByTitle() {
    let sortByAttribute = this.state.sorting === 'asc' ? "title" :
"-title";
    let unsortedBooks = Object.assign([], this.state.books);
    unsortedBooks.map((book) => book.title = book.title.
toUpperCase());
    console.log("unsortedBooks");
    console.log(unsortedBooks[0].title);
    console.log("this.state.books");
    console.log(this.state.books[0].title);
  }
```

```
unsortedBooks
THE DA VINCI CODE
this.state.books
THE DA VINCI CODE
```

"As you can see, even after using `Object.assign`, `this.state.books` was still mutated. Actually, this has nothing to do with React as such. It is due to the way JavaScript passes references of arrays and objects around. However, due to this, if we have arrays and objects in our deeply nested state, it becomes hard to prevent mutations." Mike further explained.

"Do we always have to perform a deep copy of the state object to be on the safer side?" Shawn asked.

"Well, deep copies can be expensive and sometimes hard to achieve with deeply nested state. Fortunately, React provides the Update addon with immutability helpers, which we can use to solve this issue." added Mike.

"While using immutability helpers, we need to answer the following three questions:"

- What needs to be changed?
- Where it needs to be changed?
- How it needs to be changed?

"In this case, we need to change the `this.state` to display the sorted books."

"The second question is that where should the mutation happen inside `this.state`? The mutation should happen in `this.state.books`."

"The third question is that how should the mutation happen? Are we going to delete something or add any new element or restructure existing elements? In this case, we want to sort the elements as per some criterion."

"The Update addon accepts two parameters. The first parameter is the object that we want to mutate. The second parameter tells us where and how should the mutation take place in the first parameter. In this case, we want to mutate `this.state`. In `this.state`, we want to update the books with the sorted books. Therefore, our code will look similar to the following:"

```
Update(this.state, { books: { sortedBooks }})
```

Available commands

The Update addon provides different commands to perform the mutations in arrays and objects. The syntax of these commands is inspired by MongoDB's query language.

"Most of these commands operate on array objects allowing us to push in an array or unshift an element from the array. It also supports replacing the target entirely using the set command. Other than this, it also provides the merge command to merge new keys with an existing object." Mike explained.

"Shawn, my favorite command provided by this addon is apply. It takes a function and applies that function to the current value of the target that we want to modify. It gives more flexibility to make changes in the complex data structures. It's also a hint for your next task. Try to use it to sort the books by title without mutating." Mike challenged.

"Sure. Here you go," said Shawn.

```
// src/App.js

import Update from 'react-addons-update';

_sortByTitle() {
  let sortByAttribute = this.state.sorting === 'asc' ? "title" :
"-title";
  console.log("Before sorting");
  console.log(this.state.books[0].title);
  let newState = Update(this.state,
                        { books: { $apply: (books) => { return books.
sort(sortBy(sortByAttribute)) } },
                          sorting: { $apply: (sorting) => { return
sorting === 'asc' ? 'desc' : 'asc' } } });
  console.log("After sorting");
  console.log(this.state.books[0].title);
  this.setState(newState);
}
```

```
Before sorting
The Da Vinci Code
After sorting
The Da Vinci Code
```

"Perfect, Shawn. Using the Update addon makes it very easy to manage complex state without actually mutating it."

 Check https://facebook.github.io/immutable-js/ docs/ for a complete solution for using immutable data structures in JavaScript.

Cloning components

"Shawn, props are also immutable in React. In most of the cases, the child component just uses props passed by the parent component. However, sometimes we want to extend the incoming props with some new data before rendering the child component. It's a typical use case to update styles and CSS classes. React provides an addon to clone a component and extending its props. It's called the **cloneWithProps** addon." said Mike.

"Mike, that addon is deprecated. I had looked at it in the past and React has deprecated it. It also has lot of issues related to refs of the child component not getting passed to the newly-cloned child components," Shawn informed.

"True. However, React also has a top-level `React.cloneElement` API method, which allows us to clone and extend a component. It has a very simple API and it can be used instead of the cloneWithProps addon." Mike explained.

```
React.cloneElement(element, props, ...children);
```

"This method can be used to clone the given element and merge the new props with existing props. It replaces existing children with new children. Therefore, we have to keep this in mind while dealing with the child components."

"The `cloneElement` function also passes ref of the old child component to the newly-cloned component. Therefore, if we have any callbacks based on refs, they will continue to work even after cloning."

"Shawn, here is your next challenge. We show listing of books in our app. In fact, in all of our apps, we show the listing of other things such as products, items, and so on. We want to show the rows with alternate colors in all of these listings instead of just white background. As the code for this feature will be the same across all the apps, I am thinking about creating a separate component that will accept rows as input and render them with alternate colors. Such components can be used in all of our apps. I think that you can make use of `React.cloneElement` for this." Mike explained the next task.

"Sounds like a good idea to extract this as a separate component. We need it in almost all the apps. Our QA was complaining about the lack of colors in our search app yesterday." Shawn remembered.

"Let's add some alternate colors then." Mike chuckled.

"First, let's see how we are displaying books currently."

```
// src/App.js

render() {
    let tabStyles = {paddingTop: '5%'};
    return (
      <div className='container'>
        <div className="row" style={tabStyles}>
          <div className="col-lg-8 col-lg-offset-2">
            <h4>Open Library | Search any book you want!</h4>
            <div className="input-group">
```

```
                <input type="text" className="form-control"
placeholder="Search books..." ref='searchInput'/>
                <span className="input-group-btn">
                    <button className="btn btn-default" type="button"
onClick={this._performSearch}>Go!</button>
                </span>
            </div>
          </div>
        </div>
        {this._displaySearchResults()}
      </div>
    );
  },

_displaySearchResults() {
    if(this.state.searching) {
      return <Spinner />;
    } else if(this.state.searchCompleted) {
      return (
        <BookList
            searchCount={this.state.totalBooks}
            _sortByTitle={this._sortByTitle}>
          {this._renderBooks()}
        </BookList>
      );
    }
  }

_renderBooks() {
    return this.state.books.map((book, idx) => {
      return (
        <BookRow key={idx}
                title={book.title}
                author_name={book.author_name}
                edition_count={book.edition_count} />
      );
    })
  },

})
  }
```

"The `BookList` component just renders the rows passed to it as it is using `this.props.children`."

```
// BookList component

var BookList = React.createClass({
  render() {
    return (
      <div className="row">
        <div className="col-lg-8 col-lg-offset-2">
          <span className='text-center'>
            Total Results: {this.props.searchCount}
          </span>
          <table className="table table-stripped">
            <thead>
              <tr>
                <th><a href="#" onClick={this.props._
sortByTitle}>Title</a></th>
                <th>Author</th>
                <th>No. of Editions</th>
              </tr>
            </thead>
            <tbody>
              {this.props.children}
            </tbody>
          </table>
        </div>
      </div>
    );
  }
});
```

"Mike, I am naming the component `RowAlternator`. The `RowAlternator` component will get the dynamic array of children rows and it will render them with alternate colors. We can pass multiple colors to `RowAlternator` too. In this way, the client code using this component can control the colors that they want to use as alternate colors."

"Sounds good, Shawn. I think this much API is enough for now."

```
// RowAlternator component

import React from 'react';

var RowAlternator = React.createClass({
```

```
    propTypes: {
      firstColor: React.PropTypes.string,
      secondColor: React.PropTypes.string
    },

    render() {
      return (
        <tbody>
          { this.props.children.map((row, idx) => {
              if (idx %2 == 0) {
                return React.cloneElement(row, { style: { background:
this.props.firstColor }});
              } else {
                return React.cloneElement(row, { style: { background:
this.props.secondColor }});
              }
          })
        }
        </tbody>
      )
    }
});

module.exports = RowAlternator;
```

"As we don't know how many children elements we will get in `RowAlternator`, we will just iterate over all of them and set style with alternate colors. We are also using `React.cloneElement` here to clone the passed child and extend its style prop with appropriate background color."

"Let's change our `BookList` component now in order to use `RowAlternator`."

```
// BookList component

import RowAlternator from '../src/RowAlternator';

var BookList = React.createClass({
  render() {
    return (
      <div className="row">
        <div className="col-lg-8 col-lg-offset-2">
          <span className='text-center'>
            Total Results: {this.props.searchCount}
          </span>
```

```
          <table className="table table-stripped">
            <thead>
              <tr>
                <th><a href="#" onClick={this.props._
sortByTitle}>Title</a></th>
                <th>Author</th>
                <th>No. of Editions</th>
              </tr>
            </thead>
            <RowAlternator firstColor="white" secondColor="lightgrey">
              {this.props.children}
            </RowAlternator>
          </table>
        </div>
      </div>
    );
  }
});
```

"We are all set. The listing now shows alternate colors as we wanted, as shown in the following image:"

Open Library | Search any book you want!		
Dan Brown		Go!
Total Results: 678		

Title	Author	No. of Editions
The Da Vinci Code	Dan Brown	35
Angels & Demons	Dan Brown	35
Deception point	Dan Brown	19
Digital fortress	Dan Brown	19
The Lost Symbol	Dan Brown	10

"Perfect, Shawn. As you already noticed, using `React.cloneElement` makes sense when we are building a component with dynamic children, where we don't have control on the render method of these children, but want to extend their props based on some criteria." Mike was happy.

Helpers for testing React apps

"Shawn, we have not added any tests for our app yet, however, the time has come to start slowly adding test coverage. With the Jest library and Test Utilities addon, it becomes very easy to set up and start testing the React apps." Mark explained the next task.

"I have heard about Jest. Isn't it a testing library by Facebook?" Shawn asked.

Setting up Jest

"Yes. It's built on top of Jasmine. It's very easy to set up. First, we have to install the `jest-cli` and `babel-jest` packages."

```
npm install jest-cli --save-dev
npm install babel-jest --save-dev
```

"After that, we need to configure `package.json`, as follows:"

```
{
  ...
  "scripts": {
    "test": "jest"
  },

  "jest": {
    "scriptPreprocessor": "<rootDir>/node_modules/babel-jest",
      "unmockedModulePathPatterns": [
          "<rootDir>/node_modules/react",
          "<rootDir>/node_modules/react-dom",
          "<rootDir>/node_modules/react-addons-test-utils",
          "<rootDir>/node_modules/fbjs"
      ],
    "testFileExtensions": ["es6", "js", "jsx"],
    "moduleFileExtensions": ["js", "json", "es6"]
  }
  ...
}
```

"By default, Jest mocks all modules, however, here we are telling Jest not to mock React and the related libraries. We are also specifying the extensions for our test file that will be identified by Jest as test files."

"Create a __test__ folder, where we will be adding our tests. Jest will run the tests from files in this folder. Let's add an empty file too. We have to make sure that the file should end with -test.js so that Jest will pick up it to run the tests." Mike explained.

```
mkdir __test__
touch __test__/app-test.js
```

"Now let's verify that we can run the tests from the command line."

```
$ npm test


> react-addons-examples@0.0.1 test /Users/prathamesh/Projects/sources/
reactjs-by-example/chapter7
> jest


Using Jest CLI v0.7.1
PASS __tests__/app-test.js (0.007s)
```

 You should see an output that is similar to the preceding output. It may change based on the Jest version. Consult https://facebook.github.io/jest/docs/getting-started.html to set up Jest, in case of any issues.

"Shawn, we are all set with Jest. It's time to start writing the tests now. We will test whether the top-level App component gets mounted correctly. However, first, we need to understand a bit more about using Jest," said Mike.

"By default, Jest mocks all the modules that are required in a test file. Jest does this to isolate the module that is under test from all the other modules. In this case, we want to test the App component. If we just require it, then Jest will provide a mocked version of App."

```
// app-test.js

const App = require('App'); // Mocked by Jest
```

"As we we want to test the `App` component itself, we need to specify Jest not to mock it. Jest provides the `jest.dontmock()` function for this purpose."

```
// app-test.js

jest.dontmock('./../src/App'); // Tells Jest not to mock App.
const App = require('App');
```

 Check `https://facebook.github.io/jest/docs/automatic-mocking.html` for more details about automatic mocking feature of Jest.

"Next up, we will add imports for the React and TestUtils addon."

```
// app-test.js

jest.dontMock('../src/App');
const App = require('../src/App');

import React from 'react';
import ReactDOM from 'react-dom';
import TestUtils from 'react-addons-test-utils';
```

"The TestUtils addon provides utility functions to render the components, finding sub-components in rendered components and mimicking events on the rendered component. It helps in testing both the structure and behavior of the React components." Mike added.

Testing structure of React components

"We will start with the `renderIntoDocument` function. This function renders the given component into a detached DOM node in the document. It returns `ReactComponent`, which can be used for further testing."

```
// app-test.js

describe('App', () => {
  it('mounts successfully', () => {
    let app = TestUtils.renderIntoDocument(<App />);
    expect(app.state.books).toEqual([]);
    expect(app.state.searching).toEqual(false);
  })
});
```

"We rendered the `App` component in DOM and asserted that initially books and searching state are being set correctly." Mike explained.

"Mike, this is awesome. We are not testing real DOM, but testing the React components instead."

"Yes. The TestUtils addon comes with finder methods that can be used to find the child components in a given component tree. They are useful to find the child components such as input box and submit button and simulate click events or change events."

- `findAllInRenderedTree(tree, predicate function)`: This is useful for finding all the components in a given tree that returns the truth value for the predicate function.

- `scryRenderedDOMComponentsWithClass(tree, className)`: This is useful for finding all the DOM components with a given class name.

- `findRenderedDOMComponentWithClass(tree, className)`: Instead of finding all the DOM components with a given class, this method expects that only one such component is present. It throws an exception if there are multiple components with a given class name.

- `scryRenderedDOMComponentsWithTag(tree, tagName)`: It's similar to finding the DOM components with the class name, however, instead of class name, it finds the components based on a given tag name.

- `findRenderedDOMComponentWithTag(tree, tagName)`: Instead of finding all the components with a given tag, it expects that only one such component is present. It also throws exception when more than one such components exists.

- `scryRenderedComponentsWithType(tree, componentType)`: This method finds all the components with a given type. It's useful to find all the composite components created by the user.

- `findRenderedComponentWithType (tree, componentType)`: This is similar to all the previous finder methods. It raises exception if more than one component with a given type is present.

Testing behavior of React components

"Let's use these functions to assert that the search for books starts when a user enters a search term and clicks the **Submit** button. We will simulate the event of entering search term by the user." said Mike.

```
// app-test.js

it('starts searching when user enters search term and clicks submit',
() => {
```

```
    let app = TestUtils.renderIntoDocument(<App />);

    let inputNode = TestUtils.findRenderedDOMComponentWithTag(app,
'input');
    inputNode.value = "Dan Brown";
    TestUtils.Simulate.change(inputNode);
    let submitButton = TestUtils.findRenderedDOMComponentWithTag(app,
'button');
    TestUtils.Simulate.click(submitButton);
    expect(app.state.searching).toEqual(true);
    expect(app.state.searchCompleted).toEqual(false);
})
```

"We render the `App` component, find the input node, set the value of the input node to the search term, and simulate the change event using `TestUtils.Simulate()`. This function simulates the given event dispatch on a DOM node. The `Simulate` function has a method for every event that React understands. Therefore, we can simulate all events such as change, click, and so on. We can test the user behavior using this method," Mike explained.

"Got it. Therefore, after changing the search term, we click the submit button and verify that the state gets updated as per our expectations," informed Shawn.

"Yes, Shawn. Now, can you check whether the Spinner is shown once the user clicks the **Submit** button? You can use one of the finder method that we discussed earlier." Mike explained the next task.

"Yes. Once the component state changes after clicking the **Submit** button, we can search the rendered component tree to see whether the Spinner component is present or not."

```
// app-test.js

// __tests__/app-test.js

import Spinner from './../../src/Spinner';

it('starts searching when user enters search term and clicks submit',
() => {
    let app = TestUtils.renderIntoDocument(<App />);
    let inputNode = TestUtils.findRenderedDOMComponentWithTag(app,
'input');
    inputNode.value = "Dan Brown";
    TestUtils.Simulate.change(inputNode);
    let submitButton = TestUtils.findRenderedDOMComponentWithTag(app,
'button');
    TestUtils.Simulate.click(submitButton);
```

```
    expect(app.state.searching).toEqual(true);
    expect(app.state.searchCompleted).toEqual(false);
    let spinner = TestUtils.findRenderedComponentWithType(app,
Spinner);
    expect(spinner).toBeTruthy();
  }),
```

"We are using `TestUtils.findRenderedComponentWithType` here to check whether Spinner is present in the tree rendered by the `App` component or not. However, before adding this assertion, we need to import the Spinner component at the top of the test file as `findRenderedComponentWithType` expects a second argument to be a React component."

"Excellent, Shawn. As you can see, the testing behavior of the React component becomes very easy with the `TestUtils.Simulate` and `finder` methods." Mike explained.

 Note that we have not added a test to asynchronously load the books from Open Library API as it is out of the scope of this chapter.

Shallow rendering

"Shawn, TestUtils also provides one more way to test the components in an isolated fashion using the Shallow rendering. Shallow rendering allows us render the top-level component and assert the facts about the return value of it's render method. It does not render children components or instantiate them. Therefore, our tests are not affected by the behavior of the children components. Shallow rendering also does not require a DOM, unlike the previous methods, where we rendered the component in a detached DOM," Mike explained.

```
    let renderer = TestUtils.createRenderer();
```

"This creates a shallow renderer object, in which we will render the component that we want to test. Shallow renderer has a render method similar to `ReactDOM.render`, which can be used to render the component."

```
    let renderer = TestUtils.createRenderer();
    let result = renderer.render(<App />);
```

"After render method is called, we should call `renderer.getRenderedOutput`, which returns the shallowly rendered output of rendering the component. We can start asserting facts about the component on the output of `getRenderedOutput`."

"Let's see the output we get from `getRenderedOutput`."

```
let renderer = TestUtils.createRenderer();
let result = renderer.render(<App />);
result = renderer.getRenderOutput();
console.log(result);

// Output of console.log(result)

Object {
  '$$typeof': Symbol(react.element),
  type: 'div',
  key: null,
  ref: null,
  props:
   Object {
     className: 'container',
     children: Array [ [Object], undefined ] },
  _owner: null,
  _store: Object {} }
```

"As you can see, based on the rendered output, we can assert the facts about props of the current component. However, if we want to test anything about children component, we need to explicitly reach out to them through `this.props.children[0].props.children[1].props.children`."

"This makes it hard to test the behavior of the children components using shallow rendering. However, it's useful for testing small components in an isolated way as it does not get affected by children component due to shallow rendering," said Mike.

Summary

In this chapter, we started with understanding the React addons and how to use them. We used immutability helpers and test utility functions provided by the addons. We also looked into how to clone the components.

In the next chapter, we will make our React app more performant. You will be learning about addons that will improve the performance of the React apps. Specifically, you will learn how to measure the performance of our apps and how React can make faster updates without changing most of the UI.

Let's make our React apps faster!

8
Performance of React Apps

In the previous chapter, we learned to use various React add-ons. We saw add-ons ranging from immutability helpers to test utilities.

In this chapter, we will look at React performance tools that can improve the performance of our React apps. In particular, we will be using the PERF add-on, `PureRenderMixin` and `shouldComponentUpdate`. We will also look at some of the gotchas that needs to be considered while using the performance tools provided by React.

Performance of React apps

"Hey Mike, I have few questions for you today. I have been thinking about our search app over the weekend. Do you have some time to discuss them?" Shawn asked.

"Sure, but let me get some coffee first. Okay, I am ready now. Shoot!" said Mike.

"I have few questions about the performance of React apps. I know React is very good at re-rendering the component tree whenever the state changes. React has made it very easy for me to understand and reason my code. However, does it not hamper the performance? Re-rendering seems like a very costly affair, especially when re-rendering large component trees." Shawn asked.

"Shawn, the re-rendering can be expensive. Nevertheless, React is smart about it. It only renders the part that is changed. It does not need to re-render everything on the page. It's also smart at keeping the DOM manipulation as least as possible."

"How is that possible? How does it know which part of the page is changed? Does it not depend on user interactions or incoming states and props?" questioned Shawn.

"The virtual DOM comes to the rescue here. It does all the heavy lifting of keeping track of what changed and helping React make only minimal changes to the real DOM." Mike explained.

Virtual DOM

"Shawn, React uses virtual DOM to keep track of what has changed in the real DOM. It's concept is very easy to understand. React always keeps a copy of the representation of the actual DOM in memory. Whenever something changes, such as some state manipulation, it calculates another copy of the DOM that will be generated with new state and props. Then it calculates the difference between the original copy of the virtual DOM and the new copy of the virtual DOM. This difference results in minimal operations on the real DOM that can take the current DOM to a new stage. In this way, React does not have to do major changes when something changes." Mike explained.

"But isn't the diff calculation expensive?" asked Shawn.

"It's not expensive when you compare it with actual DOM operations. Manipulation of DOM is always expensive. The comparison of virtual DOM occurs in JavaScript code, so it is always faster than doing manual DOM operations." said Mike.

"Another advantage of this approach is that once React knows what operations are needed to be performed on DOM, it does them in a single batch. Therefore, when we render a list of 100 elements, instead of appending one element at a time, React will do minimal DOM operations to insert these 100 elements on the page." Mike explained.

"I am impressed!" Shawn exclaimed .

"You will be more impressed. Let me actually show you what I mean. Let's use the PERF add-on from React and actually see what we discussed in real time."

The PERF addon

"Let's start with installing the PERF addon."

```
$ npm install react-addons-perf --save-dev
```

"We need this add-on only in the development mode. This is an important point to remember because in production, we don't need the debugging information as it may make our app slow." informed Mike.

"Shawn, the PERF add-on can be used to see what changes React is doing with the DOM, where is it spending time while rendering our app, is it wasting some time while rendering, and so on. This information can then be used to improve the performance of the app." said Mike.

"Let's start by exposing the PERF add-on as a global object. We can use it in the browser console while our app is running to see how React is making changes as per the user interactions." explained Mike.

```js
// index.js
import ReactDOM from 'react-dom';
import React from 'react';
import App from './App';
import Perf from 'react-addons-perf';

window.Perf = Perf;

ReactDOM.render(<App />, document.getElementById('rootElement'));
```

"We have imported the PERF add-on in our `index.js` file, which is the starting point of the app. We can access the `Perf` object in the browser console as we have attached it to `window.Perf`." Mike added.

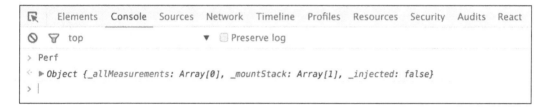

"The PERF add-on comes with methods that can help us understand what React is doing with the DOM when something changes. Let's measure some performance statistics. We will start the measurement process by calling `Perf.start()` in the browser console. After that, we will interact with the app. We will type in a query to search a book, hit submit, and the search results will be displayed. We will stop the performance measurement by calling `Perf.stop()` in the browser console. After that, let's analyze the information that we gathered." Mike explained the process.

"Let's search for books written by Dan Brown."

"Once the results are displayed, let's stop the performance measurements."

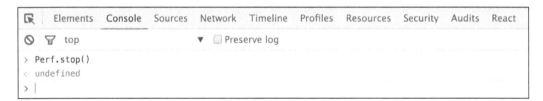

DOM operations performed by React

"Shawn, the PERF add-on can show us which DOM operations were performed by React. Let's see what manipulations React did to the DOM to render the list of books by Dan Brown." said Mike.

```
>  Perf.printDOM()
                                                                              ReactDefaultPerf.js:103
   (index)                    data-reactid            type                args
   0                          ".0"                    "set innerHTML"     "{"toIndex":2,"markup":"<di…
   1                          ".0"                    "remove"            "{"fromIndex":2}"
   2                          ".0"                    "set innerHTML"     "{"toIndex":2,"markup":"<di…
   3                          ".0.2.0.1.0.0.1.0.0"    "putListener"       "["onClick",null]"
   ▶ Array[4]
   Total time: 79.82 ms                                                       ReactDefaultPerf.js:110
   undefined
```

"The Perf.printDOM() method tells us the DOM manipulations made by React. It has made only two set innerHTML calls. First one is to render the spinner and second one is to render the list of rows. In between, we see a call to remove, which must be when the spinner was removed from the page."

"Wow, this method looks very handy as it can tell us if React is somehow doing some extra DOM manipulations." said Shawn.

"Yes, but there are more tools for the purpose analyzing the performance. Let's see how much time does React require to render each component. This can be achieved using Perf.printInclusive()." explained Mike.

Time taken to render all the components

```
>  Perf.printInclusive()
                                                                              ReactDefaultPerf.js:73
   (index)            Owner > component           Inclusive time (ms)     Instances
   0                  "<root> > App"              67.63                   2
   1                  "App > BookList"            55.84                   1
   2                  "BookList > RowAlternator"  54.13                   1
   3                  "App > BookRow"             50.22                   100
   4                  "App > Form"                10.81                   11
   Total time: 79.82 ms                                                       ReactDefaultPerf.js:80
   undefined
```

"This method prints the overall time taken to render all the components. This also included the time required to process props and set up initial state and calls to componentDidMount and componentWillMount."

"Therefore, if we have some time-intensive operation in one of these hooks, it will impact the output shown by the printInclusive function, right?" Shawn asked.

"Exactly. Though the PERF add-on provided another method — `printExclusive()` — that prints the time to taken render without these hooks, which are used to mount apps."

```
> Perf.printExclusive()
                                                                    ReactDefaultPerf.js:55
  (i. Component clas… Total inclusive… Exclusive mount… Exclusive render… Mount time per▲ Render time pe… Instances
  0  "BookRow"        50.12            50.12            12.84             0.5             0.12            100
  2  "BookList"       55.27            1.79             0.53              1.79            0.53            1
  1  "RowAlternator"  53.47            3.35             0.93              3.35            0.93            1
<- undefined
```

"But Mike, these methods are not that helpful for detecting the performance of React. I get the overall picture about what all things happened, but it does not tell me how to optimize which part." asked Shawn.

Time wasted by React

"Shawn, the PERF add-on can also tell us how much time was wasted by React and where. It is helpful in determining the parts of our app that we can optimize further." said Mike.

"What is wasted time?"

"When React re-renders a component tree, some components may not change from their previous representation. However, if they are rendered again, then React has wasted time in rendering the same output. The PERF add-on can keep track of all such time and give us a summary of how React wasted time rendering the same output as before. Let's see this in action." said Mike.

```
> Perf.printWasted()
                                                                    ReactDefaultPerf.js:96
  (index)              Owner > component        Wasted time (ms)          Instances
  0                    "App > Form"             1.7049999999999272        2
  Total time: 67.19 ms                                                    ReactDefaultPerf.js:97
<- undefined
```

"The PERF add-on tells us that it wasted time in re-rendering the `Form` component twice, but nothing was changed in the Form component, therefore, it just re-rendered everything as it is." explained Mike.

"Let's see the `Form` component to understand why it is happening."

```
// src/Form.js

import React from 'react';

export default React.createClass({
```

```
  getInitialState() {
    return { searchTerm: '' };
  },

  _submitForm() {
    this.props.performSearch(this.state.searchTerm);
  },

  render() {
    return (
      <div className="row" style={this.props.style}>
        <div>
          <div className="input-group">
            <input type="text"
                   className="form-control input-lg"
                   placeholder="Search books..."
                   onChange={ (event) => { this.setState({searchTerm:
event.target.value}) }}/>
            <span className="input-group-btn">
              <button className="btn btn-primary btn-lg"
                      type="button"
                      onClick={this._submitForm}>
                Go!
              </button>
            </span>
          </div>
        </div>
      </div>
    )
  }
}))
```

"Shawn, the `Form` component does not depend on state or props for its rendering. It renders the same output irrespective of state and props. However, we update its state when a user enters a character in the input box. Due to this, React will re-render it. Nothing is actually changed in the re-rendered output. Therefore, the PERF add-on is complaining about the wasted time." Mike explained.

"This is useful information, but this looks like an insignificant wastage, right?" Shawn asked.

"Agree. Let's make some changes so that I can show you how React can literally waste a lot of time re-rendering the same output when it shouldn't." said Mike.

"Currently, we only show the first 100 search results returned by the Open Library API. Let's change our code to show all the results on same page."

```
// src/App.js
getInitialState() {
    return { books: [],
             totalBooks: 0,
             offset: 100,
             searching: false,
             sorting: 'asc',
             page: 1,
             searchTerm: '',
             totalPages: 1
    };
}
```

"I have introduced a new state to hold the search term, total number of pages to fetch from the Open Library, and current page number being fetched."

"Now, we want to fetch all the results from the API, by default, on the same page. The API returns us the total number of books found for a query in the numFounds attribute. Based on this, we need to find the total number of pages that we need to fetch from the API."

"Also, each time maximum 100 records are returned that we have stored in state. offset already."

```
totalPages = response.numFound / this.state.offset + 1;
```

"Once we get the total number of pages, we need to keep asking for the search results for the next page until all the pages are fetched. You want to try and get this working?" asked Mike.

"Sure." said Shawn.

```
// src/App.js

// Called when user hits "Go" button.
_performSearch(searchTerm) {
   this.setState({searching: true, searchTerm: searchTerm});
   this._searchOpenLibrary(searchTerm);
},

_searchOpenLibrary(searchTerm) {
   let openlibraryURI = `https://openlibrary.org/search.json?q=${sear
chTerm}&page=${this.state.page}`;
```

```
      this._fetchData(openlibraryURI).then(this._updateState);
    },

    // called with the response received from open library API
    _updateState(response) {
      let jsonResponse = response;
      let newBooks = this.state.books.concat(jsonResponse.docs);
      let totalPages = jsonResponse.numFound / this.state.offset + 1;
      let nextPage = this.state.page + 1;

      this.setState({
        books: newBooks,
        totalBooks: jsonResponse.numFound,
        page: nextPage,
        totalPages: totalPages
      } this._searchAgain);
    },

      // Keep searching until all pages are fetched.
    _searchAgain() {
      if (this.state.page > this.state.totalPages) {
        this.setState({searching: false});
      } else {
        this._searchOpenLibrary(this.state.searchTerm);
      }
    }
}
```

"I changed the API URL to include the page parameter. Each time the response is received from API, we update the state with a new page. We also update this. state.books to include the newly fetched books. Then, the _searchAgain function gets called in the callback of the this.setState call so that it is the correct value of the next page that was set by the this.setState call." explains Shawn.

"Nice, it's an important point to remember not to call the _searchAgain function outside of the this.setState() call as it may get executed before setState() is finished.

Because if we call it outside, the _searchAgain function may use an incorrect value of this.state.page. However, as you have passed the _searchAgain function in the callback to setState, there is no chance this will happen." said Mike.

"The _searchAgain function just keeps fetching the results until all the pages are completed. In this way, we will display all the search results on the page, not just the first 100." informed Shawn.

"That's what I wanted. Good job. Let me cleanup the render method so that spinner will always be displayed at the bottom." said Mike.

```
// src/App.js
render() {
    let style = {paddingTop: '5%'};
    return (
      <div className='container'>
        <Header style={style}></Header>
        <Form style={style}
                performSearch={this._performSearch}>
        </Form>

        {this.state.totalBooks > 0 ?
         <BookList
            searchCount={this.state.totalBooks}
            _sortByTitle={this._sortByTitle}>
          {this._renderBooks()}
         </BookList>
        : null }

        { this.state.searching ? <Spinner /> : null }
      </div>
    );
}
```

"This will make sure that the spinner will be displayed until all the results are displayed. OK, all done. Now let's measure the performance again." said Mike.

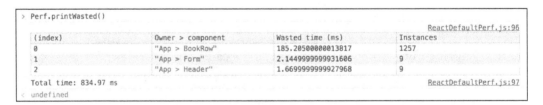

"Wow, the wasted time has increased a lot! Did Dan Brown release new books or what? So much extra time than what we saw last time?" said Shawn.

"Haha, I don't think that he released new books just now. Whenever the books on next page are fetched, we add them to the existing books and start fetching books from the next page. However, the books rendered for the previous pages are not changed at all. As we are keeping all of our state in the top-level `App` component, whenever its state changes, the whole component tree under `App` gets re-rendered. Therefore, `BookList` is rendered again. In turn, all `BookRows` are rendered again. This results in a significant amount of time getting wasted in rendering the same `BookRow` components for the previous pages again and again." said Mike.

"So each time we fetch books from a new page, all books, including the existing ones already present on page, get re-rendered again? I think just appending new book rows to the existing list is better in this case." said Shawn.

"Don't worry. We can easily get rid of this unnecessary wastage of time. React provides us a hook for short-circuiting the re-render process. It's `shouldComponentUpdate`."

The shouldComponentUpdate hook

"Shawn, `shouldComponentUpdate` is a hook that tells React whether to re-render a component or not. It's not called for initial rendering of the component. However, whenever a component is going to receive new state or props, `shouldComponentUpdate` is called before that. If the return value of this function is true, then React re-renders the component. However, if the return value is `false`, then React does not re-render the component until the next time it is called. The `componentWillUpdate` and `componentDidUpdate` hooks will also not be called in this case." Mike explained.

"Nice. Then why did our code waste so much time? Should React not use this hook to optimize it and not re-render the same `BookRow` components repeatedly?" Shawn asked.

"By default, `shouldComponentUpdate` always returns true. React does this to avoid subtle bugs. We can have mutable state or props in our code that can make `shouldComponentUpdate` to return false positives. It may return false when it should return true, resulting in the component not being re-rendered when it should. Therefore, React places the responsibility of implementing `shouldComponentUpdate` in the developer's hand." said Mike.

"Let's try to use `shouldComponentUpdate` ourselves in order to reduce the time wasted in re-rendering the same `BookRow` components." Mike added.

"This is our BookRow component as of now:"

```
// src/BookRow.js

import React from 'react';

export default React.createClass({
  render() {
    return(
      <tr style={this.props.style}>
        <td><h4>#{this.props.index}</h4></td>
        <td><h4>{this.props.title}</h4></td>
        <td><h4>{(this.props.author_name || []).join(', ')}</h4></td>
        <td><h4>{this.props.edition_count}</h4></td>
      </tr>
    );
  }
});
```

"Let's add shouldComponentUpdate to reduce unnecessary re-rendering."

```
// src/BookRow.js

import React from 'react';

export default React.createClass({
  shouldComponentUpdate(nextProps, nextState) {
    return nextProps.title !== this.props.title ||
           nextProps.author_name !== this.props.author_name ||
           nextProps.edition_count !== this.props.edition_count;
  },

  render() {
    return(
      <tr style={this.props.style}>
        <td><h4>#{this.props.index}</h4></td>
        <td><h4>{this.props.title}</h4></td>
        <td><h4>{(this.props.author_name || []).join(', ')}</h4></td>
        <td><h4>{this.props.edition_count}</h4></td>
      </tr>
    );
  }
});
```

The `shouldComponentUpdate` hook gets `nextProps` and `nextState` as arguments and we can compare them with the current state or props to make a decision whether to return true or false.

"Here, we are checking whether the title, author name, or edition count is changed or not. If any of these attributes are changed, then we will return `true`. However, if all of them are unchanged, then we will return `false`. Therefore, if none of the props are changed, the component will not get re-rendered. As the `BookRow` component only depends on props, we don't have to worry about the state change at all." added Mike.

"Now, measure the performance again and see if we got some improvements."

```
>  Perf.printWasted()
                                                                          ReactDefaultPerf.js:96
   (index)            Owner > component            Wasted time (ms)       Instances
   0                  "App > BookList"             13.224999999998545     1
   1                  "BookList > RowAlternator"   12.444999999999709     1
   2                  "App > Form"                 7.96000000001095       18
   3                  "App > Header"               1.4849999999933061     9
   Total time: 403.90 ms                                                  ReactDefaultPerf.js:97
<  undefined
```

"Awesome, we got rid of the time spent in re-rendering the `BookRow` components completely. However, we can still improve a lot. Looks like we can also get rid of the time spent re-rendering the `Form` and `Header` components, based on the preceding result. They are static components. Therefore, they should not be re-rendered at all. Shawn, that's your next challenge."

"On it."

```
// src/Header.js

import React from 'react';

export default React.createClass({
  shouldComponentUpdate(nextProps, nextState) {
    return false;
  },

  render() {
    return (
      <div className="row" style={this.props.style}>
        <div className="col-lg-8 col-lg-offset-2">
          <h1>Open Library | Search any book you want!</h1>
        </div>
      </div>
```

```
      )
    }
})

// src/Form.js

import React from 'react';

export default React.createClass({
  getInitialState() {
    return { searchTerm: '' };
  },

  shouldComponentUpdate(nextProps, nextState) {
    return false;
  },

  _submitForm() {
    this.props.performSearch(this.state.searchTerm);
  },

  render() {
    return (
      <div className="row" style={this.props.style}>
        <div>
          <div className="input-group">
            <input type="text"
                   className="form-control input-lg"
                   placeholder="Search books..."
                   onChange={(event) => { this.setState({searchTerm:
event.target.value}) }}/>
            <span className="input-group-btn">
              <button className="btn btn-primary btn-lg"
                      type="button"
                      onClick={this._submitForm}>
                Go!
              </button>
            </span>
          </div>
        </div>
      </div>
    )
  }
})
```

"Mike, we can simply return `false` from `shouldComponentUpdate` for `Header` and `Form` components as they do not depend on states or props at all for rendering!"

"Perfect find, Shawn. Make a note of such static components that do not depend on anything. They are perfect targets for just telling React to not even compare their virtual DOM as they do not need to be re-rendered at all." informed Mike.

"Right. I will keep an eye on such static parts of UI that can be extracted into smaller components." said Shawn.

"Let's now see if we got rid of some more wasted time after doing these improvements."

```
> Perf.printWasted()
                                                                      ReactDefaultPerf.js:96
  (index)                 Owner > component        Wasted time (ms)    Instances
  0                       "App > BookList"          18.22999999998865   1
  1                       "BookList > RowAlternator" 15.47000000000844   1
  Total time: 437.71 ms                                                ReactDefaultPerf.js:97
< undefined
```

"Cool! We got rid of the time wasted for re-rendering the same `Header` and `Form` components." said Mike.

"Awesome! Let me also try to get rid of the time spent on `BookList` and `RowAlternator` too." informed Shawn.

"Hold on, Shawn. Before doing this, I want to discuss about an alternative to `shouldComponentUpdate`."

PureRenderMixin

"Shawn, `PureRenderMixin` is an add-on that can be used in place of `shouldComponentUpdate`. Under the hood, it uses `shouldComponentUpdate` and compares the current props and state with the next props and states. Let's try it in our code. First, we need to install the add-on, of course." said Mike.

```
$ npm install react-addons-pure-render-mixin
```

```
// src/Header.js
```

```
import React from 'react';
import PureRenderMixin from 'react-addons-pure-render-mixin';
```

```
export default React.createClass({
```

```
    mixins: [PureRenderMixin],

        . .

        . .

})


// src/Form.js


import React from 'react';
import PureRenderMixin from 'react-addons-pure-render-mixin';


export default React.createClass({
  mixins: [PureRenderMixin],

    . .

    . .

        }
})
```

"Shawn, let's see the wasted time now that we have used `PureRenderMixin`."
said Mike.

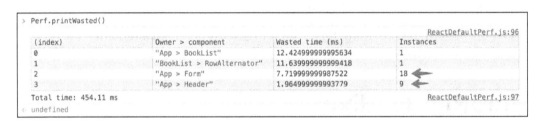

"Oh, it got worse. The `PureRenderMixin` function added the time wasted in
re-rendering `Form` and `Header` components back. What is going on, Mike?"
Shawn asked.

"Calm down! I am going to explain why this happened. The `PureRenderMixin`
compares the current props and state with the next props and state, but it does
shallow comparison. Therefore, if we are passing the state or props that contain
objects and arrays, then the shallow comparison will not return true even if they
both have the same content." Mike explained.

"However, where are we passing any complex objects or arrays to the `Header` and `Form` components? We are just passing the book data such as the name of author, edition count, and so on. We are not passing anything to `Header`, how does `PureRenderMixin` fail?" Shawn asked.

"You are forgetting style prop passed to `Header` and `Form` from the `App` component." informed Mike.

```
// src/App.js

render() {
    let style = {paddingTop: '5%'};
    return (
      <div className='container'>
        <Header style={style}></Header>
        <Form style={style}
              performSearch={this._performSearch}>
        </Form>
          ..

          ..
      </div>
)}
```

"Each time `App` gets re-rendered, a new object for style is created and sent to `Header` and `Form` in props."

```
> {paddingTop: '5%'} === {paddingTop: '5%'}
< false
>
```

The PureRenderMixin anti pattern

The `PureRenderMixin` internally implements `shouldComponentUpdate`, as follows:

```
var ReactComponentWithPureRenderMixin = {
  shouldComponentUpdate: function(nextProps, nextState) {
    return shallowCompare(this, nextProps, nextState);
  },
};
```

The `shallowCompare` function is also an add-on provided by React that is a helper function to compare the current state and props with the next state and props. It basically achieves the same thing as `PureRenderMixin`, but as it is a function, it can be used directly instead of using `PureRenderMixin`. It is especially needed when we are using ES6 classes with React." Mike explained.

"Mike, so the shallow comparison is the reason why `PureRenderMixin` is failing to detect that there is no change in the next props?" Shawn asked.

"Yes. The `shallowCompare` just iterates over the keys of objects that are being compared and returns false when the value of the key in each object is not strictly equal. Therefore, if we pass simple props, as follows, then `shallowCompare` will correctly determine that re-rendering is not required:"

```
// shallowCompare will detect correctly that props are not changed.
{ author_name: "Dan Brown",
  edition_count: "20",
  title: "Angels and Demons" }
```

"However, it will fail immediately with a prop that is an object or array."

```
{ author_name: "Dan Brown",
  edition_count: "20",
  title: "Angels and Demons",
  style: { paddingTop: '%5' } }
```

"Though `PureRenderMixin` saves us a few lines of code, it may not work all the time as we expect it to work. Especially when we have mutable state, objects, or arrays in props." said Mike.

"Got it. So we can write our own `shouldComponentUpdate` function when we have nested state or props right?", Shawn asked.

"Yes. `PureRenderMixin` and `shallowCompare` is good for simple components with simple props and states but we should take care when we are using it." Mike.

 Using mixins is discouraged in React world for various reasons. Checkout alternative approaches for `PureRenderMixin` pattern here - `https://github.com/gaearon/react-pure-render`.

Immutable data

"Mike, I have a question though. All said and done, why does `PureRenderMixin` perform shallow comparison in the first place? Should it not perform a deep comparison so that we will always have better performance?" Shawn was not very happy with `PureRenderMixin`.

"Well, there is a reason for this. Shallow comparison is very cheap. It does not take much time. Deep comparison is always expensive. Therefore, `PureRenderMixin` does shallow comparison, which is good enough for most of the simple use cases," said Mike.

"However, React does provide us an option of defining our own version of
shouldComponentUpdate as we saw earlier. We can completely short-circuit the
re-rendering process by just returning false from shouldComponentUpdate or we
can compare only those props that are required by our component."

"True, just like we had written shouldComponentUpdate for the BookRow component
right?" asked Shawn.

```
// src/BookRow.js

export default React.createClass({
  shouldComponentUpdate(nextProps, nextState) {
    return nextProps.title !== this.props.title ||
          nextProps.author_name !== this.props.author_name ||
          nextProps.edition_count !== this.props.edition_count;
  },

  render() {
    return(
      <tr style={this.props.style}>
        ..
      </tr>
    );
  }
});
```

"Exactly, Shawn. If needed, you can also perform a deep comparison as per the
requirements of your component when needed."

```
// custom deep comparison as per requirement
shouldComponentUpdate(nextProps, nextState) {
    return nextProps.book.review === props.book.review;
}
```

"Shawn, another option we have is using immutable data. Comparing immutable
data with each other is very easy as it will always create new data or objects instead
of mutating the existing ones."

```
// pseudo code
book_ids = [1, 2, 3]
new_book_ids = book_ids.push(4)
book_ids === new_book_ids # false
```

"Therefore, we just have to compare the reference of the new object with the old object, they are always same when the values are equal and they are always different when values are unequal. Therefore, if we use immutable data for our props and state, then `PureRenderMixin` will work as expected." said Mike.

Check `http://facebook.github.io/immutable-js/` as an option for using immutable data for state and props.

Summary

In this chapter, you learned about the performance tools provided by React and how to use them. We used the PERF add-on: `shouldComponentUpdate` and `PureRenderMixin`. We also saw which areas to look for when trying to improve the performance of our apps. We also studied the pitfalls while improving the performance, especially with `PureRenderMixin`. In the end, we discussed the importance and advantages of immutable data.

In the next chapter, we will look at the data model of React in detail using React Router and Flux. You will learn how to use React with other frameworks such as Backbone.

9

React Router and Data Models

In the previous chapter, we took a look at the React performance tools that can improve performance of our React apps. We explored using the PERF add-on, PureRenderMixin, and so on and took a look at some of the gotchas related to the performance tools provided by React.

In this chapter, we will take a closer look at react-router and perform routing at different levels. We will take a look at nested routing and passing around parameters, as well as see how react-router maintains history when performing routing tasks. We will also take a look at passing and using context to render React Components. Finally, we will explore data-models and mix and match them with other frameworks to use as data models in React, Backbone in this case.

In this chapter, we will cover the following topics:

- React in your apps
- Routing with react-router
- Different routing mechanism
- Setting up routing and passing around the routing context
- React and data stores/models
- Using Backbone models/collections as data stores

At the end of chapter, we will be able to start using the react-router and different routing patterns and start passing around context data in routing. We will also be able to replace parts of plain data models with the likes of Backbone.js.

A new adventure

"Hi Shawn and Mike!" exclaimed Carla.

Shawn and Mike were startled. They had just got in and were about to start their day. The past few days had been a lot of React exploration for them.

"I have some good news for you guys. We got a new project, where we need to build a cat-based interest site. Something like say – Pinterest? Users can like images and profiles of cats. They can then see and like related articles for sale, as well," continued Carla.

"Oh, nice," replied Shawn.

Shawn and Mike regrouped and started a conversation about the new project that they just heard from Carla.

"This is nice. So, I guess, we want to display a small Pinterest-style gallery of images in panel shapes?" inquired Shawn.

"Correct," continued Mike. "We also want to display the images in large scale, maybe in a modal after a user clicks on the image. Carla said she wants random cats to be featured in the footer, which should take us to a full-fledged cat display page."

"You know what, I know the perfect thing that we are going use. Let's take a look at react-router today! I also know the perfect example to start with. We are going to look at the Pinterest example from react-router at `https://github.com/rackt/react-router/tree/master/examples/pinterest`. We will then build our app on top of it."

"Nice," said Shawn. "I can see the existing example has some of the things that we discussed, such as the modal display. Let me see how the example looks."

Shawn looked at the example, which was as follows:

```
import React from 'react'
import { render } from 'react-dom'
import { browserHistory, Router, Route, IndexRoute, Link } from
'react-router'
...
const PICTURES = [
  { id: 0, src: 'http://placekitten.com/601/601' },
  { id: 1, src: 'http://placekitten.com/610/610' },
  { id: 2, src: 'http://placekitten.com/620/620' }
]
```

```
const Modal = React.createClass({
… // Modal Class implementation
  })

const App = React.createClass({
  componentWillReceiveProps(nextProps) {
// takes care of context in case of Modals
  },
  render() {
// Main render for Modal or Cat Pages
  }
})

const Index = React.createClass({
  render() {
// Index page render
  ..

        <div>
          {PICTURES.map(picture => (
            <Link key={picture.id}
              to={{
                pathname: `/pictures/${picture.id}`,
                state: { modal: true, returnTo: this.props.location.
pathname }
              }}
            >
              <img style={{ margin: 10 }} src={picture.src}
height="100" />
            </Link>
          ))}
        </div>
  .. // Usage of React Router Links
        <p><Link to="/some/123/deep/456/route">Go to some deep route</
Link></p>
      </div>
    )
  }
})

const Deep = React.createClass({
  render() {
```

```
// Render handler for some deep link
      )
    }
  })

  const Picture = React.createClass({
    render() {
      return (
        <div>
// Pictures display
          <img src={PICTURES[this.props.params.id].src} style={{ height:
'80%' }} />
        </div>
      )
    }
  })

// The actual Routing logic using Router Library.
  render((
    <Router history={browserHistory}>
      <Route path="/" component={App}>
        <IndexRoute component={Index}/>
        <Route path="/pictures/:id" component={Picture}/>
        <Route path="/some/:one/deep/:two/route" component={Deep}/>
      </Route>
    </Router>
  ), document.getElementById('example'))
```

"Looks interesting," said Shawn.

"Yeah, let's go through the components that we need to create one by one. To begin with, let's see how we are going to store our data and display the cat data across the system. Currently, the images are stored in the PICTURES constant. We would like to store more than that."

Creating Backbone models

"So, Shawn, let's go ahead and build out our cats' collection that we want to display. For the purpose of development, we are going to use cat images from lorempixel service, for example, http://lorempixel.com/600/600/cats/. This will give us a random cat image of 600 x 600 pixels."

"Next, we are going to create a store of data using different-than-normal objects. We want to explore how to embed different model flows with our React app here. In our case, let's make use of Backbone models, instead of the PICTURES constant. I know that you have already used Backbone."

"Yup, I have used it in my previous projects."

"Alright then, let's define our `Cat` model."

```
const PictureModel = Backbone.Model.extend({
  defaults: {
    src: 'http://lorempixel.com/601/600/cats/',
    name: 'Pusheen',
    details: 'Pusheen is a Cat'
  }
});
```

"Here we store the `src` for the image of a cat, its name, and some details about it. As you can see, we have provided some default values for these attributes."

"Next, let's define our `Cats` collection to all the `Cat` records."

```
const Cats = new Backbone.Collection;
Cats.add(new PictureModel({src: "http://lorempixel.com/601/600/cats/",
                                          name: Faker.Name.
findName(),
                                          details: Faker.Lorem.
paragraph()}));

Cats.add(new PictureModel({src: "http://lorempixel.com/602/600/cats/",
                                          name: Faker.Name.
findName(),
                                          details: Faker.Lorem.
paragraph()}));
...
```

"Here, we making use of the `Faker` module to create random names for the cats using `Faker.Name.findName()`, adding random description using `Faker.Lorem.paragraph()` and passing the source as needed."

"Cool," said Shawn. "Let me see how this looks now."

```
//models.js
import Backbone from 'backbone';
import Faker from 'faker';

const PictureModel = Backbone.Model.extend({
```

```
    defaults: {
      src: 'http://lorempixel.com/601/600/cats/',
      name: 'Pusheen',
      details: 'Pusheen is a Cat'
    }
  });

  const Cats = new Backbone.Collection;
  Cats.add(new PictureModel({src: "http://lorempixel.com/601/600/cats/",
  name: Faker.Name.findName(), details: Faker.Lorem.paragraph()}));
  ...
  Cats.add(new PictureModel({src: "http://lorempixel.com/606/600/cats/",
  name: Faker.Name.findName(), details: Faker.Lorem.paragraph()}));

  module.exports = {Cats, PictureModel};
```

Incorporating defined Backbone models

"Next, let's define our index with how we need the routing to be and what paths should the routing respond to. From there, we will go ahead with building our components."

"Got it."

```
  import React from 'react'
  import { render } from 'react-dom'
  import { createHistory, useBasename } from 'history'
  import { Router, Route, IndexRoute, Link } from 'react-router'
  import Backbone from 'backbone';
  import Modal from './Modal'
  import App from './App'
  import { Cats, PictureModel } from './models';
  import Picture from './Picture'
  import Sample from './Sample'
  import Home from './Home'

  const history = useBasename(createHistory)({
    basename: '/pinterest'
  });


  render((
    <Router history={history}>
```

```
    <Route path="/" component={App}>
      <IndexRoute component={Home}/>
      <Route path="/pictures/:id" component={Picture}/>
      <Route path="/this/:cid/is/:randomId/sampleroute"
  component={Sample}/>
      </Route>
    </Router>
  ), document.getElementById('rootElement'));
```

"So, the first thing I see is that we are creating a session history?"

"Correct, we are creating a session history over here. We will use it for our router."

"Here, we are using the history module's useBasename method, which provides support for running an app under a base URL, which in our case is /pinterest."

"Got it."

"Next, we are laying out how we actually want the routing to be. We wrap our router into the <Router/> component and specify different <Route/> as paths."

"This is called the **Route Configuration**, which is basically a set of rules or instructions on how to match the URLs to some React Component in order to be displayed."

"Oh, can we discuss more about this configuration, it looks intriguing."

"It sure is. First, let's see what <IndexRoute component={Home}/> does. When we land on the / page for the application, which in our case would be /pinterest, the component defined by IndexRoute gets rendered. As you might have guessed, the component to be rendered is passed in the component argument of the route. Note that this is displayed in the App component that is the base component for all."

Similar to the IndexRoute, we have different <Route/> definitions. In our example, if you see <Route path="/pictures/:id" component={Picture}/>, it shows how route is getting used, and how we are passing attributes for the same. "Here, the path attribute is a matcher expression and component attribute specifies the component that is to be displayed after the route is matched."

"Notice how the path is defined over here, it is specified as an expression."

The matching for a route based on a URL is done on the basis of three components:

- Nesting of route
- Path attribute
- Precedence of the route

Shawn began, "I got the nesting part. I see that we have arranged our routes in a nested fashion, like a tree. The route matching and building is being done on the basis of this tree-like matching structure."

"Right. Secondly, we have the path attribute. We can see examples for these:"

```
<Route path="/pictures/:id" component={Picture}/>
<Route path="/this/:cid/is/:randomId/sampleroute"
component={Sample}/>
```

"The path value is a string that acts as a regex, which can consist of the following parts:"

- `:paramName`: For example, ID, which is the param passed in the URL such as `/pictures/12`. `12` gets parsed as `param id`.

- `()`: This can be used to specify an optional path, such as `/pictures(/:id)`, this will match `/pictures` as well as `/pictures/12`.

- `*`: As in case of regular expressions, `*` can be used to match any part of the expression, until the next `/`, `?`, or `#` occurs. For example, to match all the JPEG images, we can use `/pictures/*.jpg`.

- `**`: Greedy matching, similar to `*`, but it matches greedily. For example, `/**/*.jpg` will match `/pictures/8.jpg` as well as `/photos/10.jpg`.

"Got it. Finally, what remains is the precedence? Most probably, it should use the first route that is defined in the file and satisfy the condition used to match the path?"

"Exactly," Mike exclaimed.

"Oh, before I forget, we also have a `<Redirect>` route. This can be used to match some routes to other route actions. For example, we want `/photos/12` to match `/pictures/12` instead, we can define it as code."

```
<Redirect from="/photos/:id" to="/pictures/:id" />
```

"Awesome."

"Next, let's take a look at all the things that we are importing and using, which we will define as components."

```
import React from 'react'
...
import Modal from './Modal'
import App from './App'
import { Cats, PictureModel } from './models';
import Picture from './Picture'
import Sample from './Sample'
import Home from './Home'
```

"Let's define our `App` component first, which is going to act as the container:"

```
  ..
import { Router, Route, IndexRoute, Link } from 'react-router'
import Modal from './Modal'

const App = React.createClass({
  componentWillReceiveProps(nextProps) {
    if ((
          nextProps.location.key !== this.props.location.key &&
          nextProps.location.state &&
          nextProps.location.state.modal
      )) {
      this.previousChildren = this.props.children
    }
  },

  render() {
    let { location } = this.props;
    let isModal = ( location.state && location.state.modal
      && this.previousChildren );
    return (
        <div>
          <h1>Cats Pinterest</h1>
          <div>
            {isModal ?
                this.previousChildren :
                this.props.children
            }
            {isModal && (
                <Modal isOpen={true}
                  returnTo={location.state.returnTo}>
                  {this.props.children}
                </Modal>
            )}
          </div>
        </div>
    )
  }
});

export {App as default}
```

"We aren't going to change much here, this is from the example that we have already seen."

"I see the use of location here. Is this from react-router?"

"As we saw, our `App` is wrapped into the router. The router passes in the location object from the props. The location object is actually similar to `window.location` and it is something the history module that we use defines. The `Location` object has various special attributes defined on top of it, which we are going to make use of, as follows:"

- `pathname`: The actual pathname of the URL

- `search`: The query string

- `state`: A state passed on from the react-router and tied as an object to the location

- `action`: One of the PUSH, REPLACE, or POP operations

- `key`: The unique identifier for the location

"Got it. I can see that we are making use of `props.children` we had seen before."

```
componentWillReceiveProps(nextProps) {
  if ((
        nextProps.location.key !== this.props.location.key &&
        nextProps.location.state &&
        nextProps.location.state.modal
     )) {
    this.previousChildren = this.props.children
  }
}
```

"We are storing the children and the previous screen onto the `App` object when the Modal is displayed, I guess," queried Shawn.

"Yup. We are first checking whether we are displaying a different Component by matching the key attribute of location. We then check whether the state attribute was passed on the location and whether the modal was set to true on state. We will be doing that in case of Modal display. Here's how we will pass the state onto a link:"

```
<Link … state={{ modal: true .. }}.. />
```

" We will take a look at the `Link` object when we use it for the images."

"Got it," said Shawn.

"Then I see that we are passing around the children props or rendering the previous layout, and then, displaying Modal on top of it if modal is clicked:"

```
{isModal ?
    this.previousChildren :
    this.props.children
}
{isModal && (
    <Modal isOpen={true} returnTo={location.state.
returnTo}>
        {this.props.children}
    </Modal>
)}
```

"Exactly! You are getting pretty good at this," Mike exclaimed.

"Now, let's see our main index page component, shall we?"

```
// home.js
import React from 'react'
import { Cats, PictureModel } from './models';
import { createHistory, useBasename } from 'history'
import { Router, Route, IndexRoute, Link } from 'react-router'

const Home = React.createClass({
  render() {
    let sampleCat = Cats.sample();
    return (
        <div>
          <div>
            {Cats.map(cat => (
                <Link key={cat.cid} to={`/pictures/${cat.cid}`}
state={{ modal: true, returnTo: this.props.location.pathname }}>
                    <img style={{ margin: 10 }} src={cat.get('src')}
height="100" />
                </Link>
            ))}
          </div>
          <p><Link to={`/this/${sampleCat.cid}/is/456/
sampleroute`}>{`Interesting Details about ${sampleCat.get('name')}`}</
Link></p>
        </div>
    )
  }
});

export {Home as default}
```

"So Shawn, we are first importing all the data that we generate in the `Cats` collection. We are going to loop over them and display the images with links to Modals. You can see this happening here:"

```
{Cats.map(cat => (
        <Link key={cat.cid} to={`/pictures/${cat.cid}`}
state={{ modal: true, returnTo: this.props.location.pathname }}>
            <img style={{ margin: 10 }} src={cat.get('src')}
height="100" />
        </Link>
    ))}
```

"Yup, I see that we are setting the key using `cat` object's `cid` from the backbone object. We had to attribute for the link, which is path to where it should be linked, I guess?"

"That's right. For every cat displayed, we have a unique dynamic route generated, such as `/pictures/121` and so on. Now, as we want to display the enlarged cat when we click on it, we are passing `modal: true` to state on `<Link/>`."

"We are also passing a `returnTo` attribute that is related to the current path that we obtain from the current `location.pathname`. We will be using this `returnTo` attribute from state to set up back links on components. We will display one on the Modal so that we can get back to the home page when it's clicked and the Modal will be closed."

"Got it. I see we are also defining a link for the sample cat display page here:"

```
let sampleCat = Cats.sample();
...
render(
...
        <p><Link to={`/this/${sampleCat.cid}/is/456/
sampleroute`}>{`Interesting Details about ${sampleCat.get('name')}`}</
Link></p>
...
);
```

"Yup, we are going to randomly feature a cat here. We will display the details about the cat on the sample page. Now, I want to show you how we are creating the link here:"

```
`/this/${sampleCat.cid}/is/456/sampleroute`
```

"Here, we are creating a nested random route, for example, this can match a URL, as follows:"

```
/this/123/is/456/sampleroute
```

"The 123 and 456 act as params for the location."

"Nice," followed Shawn. "Let me define the Modal? Let me reuse the one from the example."

```
import React from 'react'
import { Router, Route, IndexRoute, Link } from 'react-router'

const Modal = React.createClass({
  styles: {
    position: 'fixed',
    top: '20%',
    right: '20%',
    bottom: '20%',
    left: '20%',
    padding: 20,
    boxShadow: '0px 0px 150px 130px rgba(0, 0, 0, 0.5)',
    overflow: 'auto',
    background: '#fff'
  },

  render() {
    return (
      <div style={this.styles}>
        <p><Link to={this.props.returnTo}>Back</Link></p>
        {this.props.children}
      </div>
    )
  }
})

export {Modal as default}
```

"That's simple and straightforward, Shawn. We also need to define how we display the pictures. Let's define that."

```
import React from 'react'
import { Cats, PictureModel } from './models';

const Picture = React.createClass({
  render() {
```

```
        return (
            <div>
                <img src={Cats.get(this.props.params.id).get('src')}
    style={{ height: '80%' }} />
            </div>
        )
    }
});
```

```
    export {Picture as default}
```

"To display the cat and fetch details about it, we are using the ID that we receive from params. These are sent to us on the params prop. We are then fetching the ID from the `Cats` collection."

```
    Cats.get(this.props.params.id)
```

"Using the `id` prop, recall how we were sending the ID on the cat link that we defined as follows"

```
    <Route path="/pictures/:id" component={Picture}/>
```

"Finally, let's take a look at how the sample component is used to display the cat information from the example:"

```
    import React from 'react'
    import { Cats, PictureModel } from './models';
    import { createHistory, useBasename } from 'history'
    import { Router, Route, IndexRoute, Link } from 'react-router'

    const Sample = React.createClass({
      render() {
        let cat = Cats.get(this.props.params.cid);
        return (
            <div>
                <p>CID for the Cat: {this.props.params.cid}, and Random ID:
    {this.props.params.randomId}</p>
                <p>Name of this Cat is: {cat.get('name')}</p>
                <p>Some interesting details about this Cat:</p>
                <p> {cat.get('details')} </p>
                </p>
            </div>
        )
      }
    });
```

```
    export {Sample as default};
```

"With this, it looks like we are done! Let's see how it looks, shall we?"

"The index page looks neat."

"Next, let's see how the Modal and the links look with the URL."

"The cat sure looks nice," chuckled Shawn.

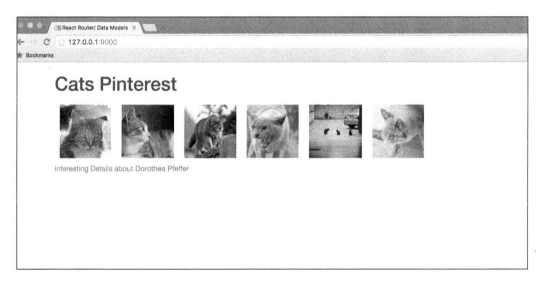

"Haha, yes."

 Notice the URL. On clicking, the modal link changed to the one on the anchor tag. We are on the same page and the modal is displayed.

"Finally, we have the sample page, where we display details of the cat. Let's see how it looks:"

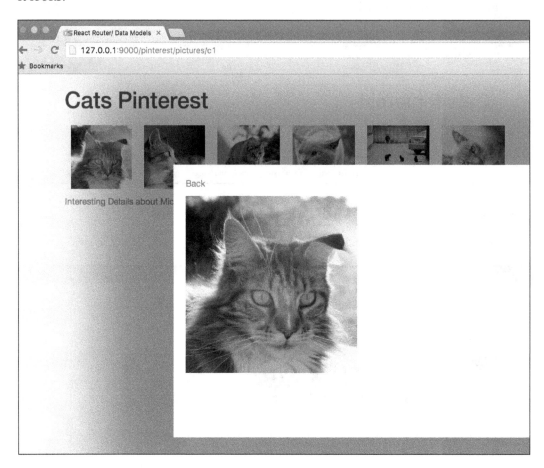

"Awesome!"

Data models and Backbone

"Shawn, I wanted to discuss how we used Backbone models here or how we are storing the data. We moved from the following code to make use of Backbone collections. This helped us to define our data in a better way:"

```
PICTURES =[{array of objects}]
```

"However, if you notice, we ended up defining a static collection of objects. Along with that, this collection was global and required to be passed around."

"That is true. I also noticed that we had a fixed `state` in a global fashion for the data. I believe, we could have not done much there. If we updated, the `Views` would still remain the same?"

"Exactly! What's happening in our case is that we are sending and using/modifying the data in a fixed fashion, globally. Any updates to this data in a different part of the application would not affect how our views were displayed or even the data that was already being accessed in different components would not change. For example, consider that the `Home` component changed the `Cats` constant. First of all, it would not sync the changes with Sample, Modal, or other components."

"Secondly, the change in the `Home` component to the `Cats` collection would not even change the `Home` component's display!"

"Ah, this is pretty tricky. I guess, we would end up storing all of this collection state in a global component state, such as the `App` component, which is rendered only once," followed Shawn.

"Yes, we could do that. The problem in that case would be that we would need to manually maintain the state and update the state from the children components to the `App` components, and so forth. Imagine having to change the state for a cat on click, for example, someone faves an image of a cat. The event would take place on the `Picture` component and we would need to manually propagate the event to `Home` or `Modal` first and then to `App` in order to actually update the global collection."

"That would not be good. I believe this would be hard to track and debug as well."

"That's right. In our next refactoring, we will try to change this approach and limit it to, say, the `App`. In the longer run, we would try out Flux."

"Oh, right, I have heard about it. It's for passing around or accessing data and managing changes in data via events or something?"

"Umm, not exactly, it helps us to streamline the data flow in a unidirectional flow. The state maintained is propagated to the components and they update as required. Events, such as having a cat, may change the data store, which in turn changes the components."

"Anyway, I just wanted to give you an idea about this and why we will explore Flux later. For now, our solution works as expected."

The day was coming to an end. It has been another interesting day at Adequate LLC. Shawn and Mike had collaborated and build a simple app using react-router and mixing Backbone models with it.

Summary

In this chapter, we built a simple Pinterest-like app, making use of react-router and taking a closer look at it while performing routing at different levels. We also took a look at nested routing, passing around parameters, how the react-router maintains history, and so on, when performing the routing tasks. We took a look at how to pass and use the context to render the React components and mix Backbone models to maintain the Cats display data.

In the next chapter, we will explore adding animation to content and some other display goodies on top of the existing app.

10
Animation

In the previous chapter, we took a look at react-router and performed routing at different levels. We also looked at nested routing, passing around parameters, and how react-router maintains history when performing the routing tasks. We learned about passing around context and using context to render React components. We explored data models and mixed and matched them with other frameworks to use as data models in React-like Backbone, and were introduced to Flux.

In this chapter, we are going to explore a fun React add-on, Animation. We will start off by continuing with our Cat Pinterest application and enhancing it to support starring and sharing the data to update the views. We will then explore adding handlers for animation. We will see how components get wrapped for animation and how React adds the handlers for different events. We will also explore different events and how we can easily enhance our application in order to create stunning effects.

In this chapter, we will cover the following topics:

- Making changes to the data flow and passing data from react-router links
- Animation in React
- CSS transitions
- Transition groups
- Transition handlers
- Animating our dynamic component

At the end of chapter, we will be able to start animating our React components for different actions such as adding new content, changing data and position, and so on. We will also be able to add handlers for different types of events and explore different animation options out there, other than core animation add-on.

Fun stuff at Adequate LLC!

"Hi Shawn and Mike!" Carla joined Mike and Shawn in their conversation.

The day before, Carla had asked them to build a Pinterest-style application for cats for one of their clients.

"How are things going today?" she enquired.

"All good, Carla. Shawn, do you want to show Carla what we built yesterday?"

"Sure."

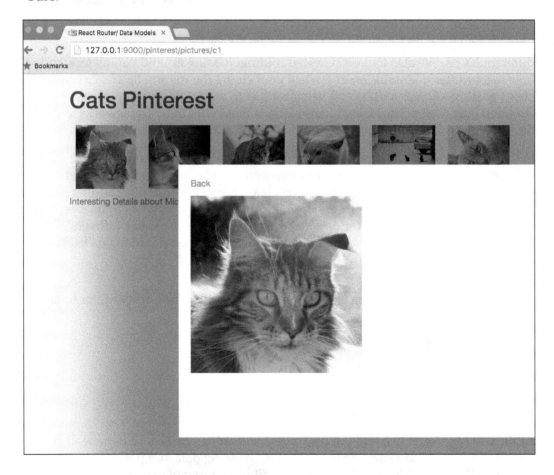

"That looks nice! Are we adding button for faving/starring of cats next?"

"Yes, we were just getting ready for that."

"Cool. The client called yesterday. What they want along with displaying the cats is to show a stream of cats being updated on the screen. This is going to happen when someone faves a cat so that we show it to other users."

"Got it. We will start working on it and simulate addition of cats to appear on the screen to start with."

"Awesome, I will leave you both to it."

Model updates

"So Shawn, instead of using the Backbone collection in an isolated fashion, let's move it to a class to manage adding of new cats randomly and provide it with some other utilities, as follows:"

```
const PictureModel = Backbone.Model.extend({
  defaults: {
    src: 'http://lorempixel.com/601/600/cats/',
    name: 'Pusheen',
    details: 'Pusheen is a Cat',
    faved: false
  }
});
```

"Our `PictureModel` stays the same. We are adding a new `faved` attribute here to maintain state about whether the cat was faved by the user or not.

"We will call this new class of ours `CatGenerator`, which will provide the component that we use to display the cats, with the data to display, fetch, and add new cats."

"Got it. Want me to give it a try?"

"Sure."

```
import Backbone from 'backbone';
import Faker from 'faker';
import _ from 'underscore';
...

class CatGenerator {
  constructor() {
    this.Cats = new Backbone.Collection;
    [600, 601, 602, 603, 604, 605].map( (height)=>{
      this.createCat(height, 600);
```

```
      })
    }

    createCat(height = _.random(600, 650), width = 600) {
      console.log('Adding new cat');
      this.Cats.add(new PictureModel({
        src: `http://lorempixel.com/${height}/${width}/cats/`,
        name: Faker.Name.findName(),
        details: Faker.Lorem.paragraph()
      }));
    }
  }
```

"Nice Shawn."

"Thanks. I moved `createCat` as a method of its own so that we can add cats to the collection on the fly. I am just adding a random one right now, taking a random height of 600-650 and a random width to create a new `PictureModel` instance."

"Also, to start with, I am creating `cats` collection as an attribute on the class. Next, I have added six cats to begin with."

"Cool. We are now going to start changing its use in our Components."

Remember that we are going to update the components when new data comes in. Easy way to do this is to start storing the `CatGenerator` as a state object on the `Home` component.

"Let's start defining and changing our `Home` component, as follows:"

```
class Home extends React.Component {
  constructor() {
    super();
    this.timer = null;
    this.state = {catGenerator: new CatGenerator()};
  }

  componentDidMount() {
    this.timer = setInterval(::this.generateCats, 1000);
  }

  generateCats() {
    let catGenerator = this.state.catGenerator;
    catGenerator.createCat();
    clearInterval(this.timer);
```

```
      this.timer = setInterval(::this.generateCats, catGenerator.
   randRange());

      this.setState({catGenerator: catGenerator});
   }
   ...
```

"So, what we are doing here is creating a timer to track time intervals. We are going to use a random time interval to simulate the addition of a new stream of cats here."

"Got it," followed up Shawn.

"To do this, I have added the `generateCats()` method. In our `componentDidMount`, we are adding and setting the timer to call this method after the first creation."

"In the method itself, I have added clearing of the old interval and we are calling the `catGenerator.createCat()` method to actually create the cat from our `CatGenerator` class."

"We are then resetting the timer and setting a new one, based on a random time interval. I added the `catGenerator.randRange()` method to generate the random time interval. Here's how it looks in the `CatGenerator` class:"

```
randRange() {
    return _.random(5000, 10000);
   }
```

"Got it. This should be creating a new stream of cats in the range of 5-10 seconds."

"Next, let's take a look at how our render method looks. I am going to add a star next to the cats."

```
render() {
    let Cats = this.state.catGenerator.Cats;

    return (
        <div>
          <div>

                {Cats.map(cat => (
                    <div key={cat.cid} style={{float: 'left'}}>
                      <Link to={`/pictures/${cat.cid}`}
                            state={{ modal: true, returnTo: this.props.
   location.pathname, cat: cat }}>
                        <img style={{ margin: 10 }} src={cat.get('src')}
   height="100"/>
                      </Link>
```

```
                              <span key={`${cat.cid}`} className="fa fa-star"></
span>
                        </div>
                  ))}


             </div>
          </div>
      )
    }
```

"There are two changes that I am doing here. First of all, I added the star, which is unfaved by default."

```
                              <span key={`${cat.cid}`} className="fa fa-star"></
span>
```

"Secondly, I started passing the cat object on the modal link's state."

```
                    <Link to={`/pictures/${cat.cid}`}
                          state={{ modal: true,
                                    returnTo: this.props.location.
pathname,

                                    cat: cat }}>
```

"In our `PictureModel` box, we previously had the access to the global collection of cats. From now on, that won't be the case and we would need the cat object to be passed to the `Picture` component."

"That's neat, we are able to pass the objects too, to the component from a router `<Link/>` object."

"Yup, let's go ahead and change the picture component in order for it to work properly with this new change in passing the data. Our `Modal` stays the same:"

```
const Modal = React.createClass({
   styles: {
...
    },

    render() {
       return (
         <div style={this.styles}>
           <p><Link to={this.props.returnTo}>Back</Link></p>
           {this.props.children}
         </div>
       )
```

```
      }
   })
   ...
   export {Modal as default}
```

"The `Picture` component now starts using the cat object."

```
   import React from 'react'
   import { PictureModel } from './models';

   const Picture = React.createClass({
     render() {
       let { location } = this.props;
       let cat = location.state.cat;
       console.log(this.props);
       return (
           <div>
             <div style={{ float: 'left', width: '40%' }}>
               <img src={cat.get('src')} style={{ height: '80%' }}/>
             </div>
             <div style={{ float: 'left', width: '60%' }}>
               <h3>Name: {cat.get('name')}.</h3>
               <p>Details: {cat.get('details')} </p>
             </div>
           </div>
       )
     }
   });

   export {Picture as default}
```

"As you can see, the cat object is received on the `location.state` object from props."

"I have extended the picture to display more details about the cat, such as the name and so on, instead of showing it on a separate page. Previously, it looked pretty blank."

"Cool, let's take a look at how it looks, shall we?"

"Nice, the stars look good. We will need to check the styles that I added for this soon."

"The modal seems to be looking good as well, and look at all these cats being generated as a stream!"

"Nice!" Mike and Shawn rejoiced.

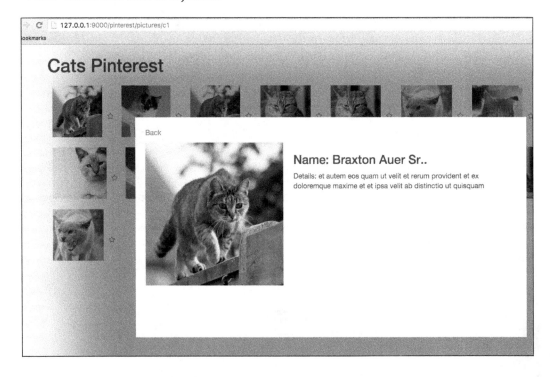

Animate

"React allows us to animate objects easily with its react-addons-css-transition-group add-on."

"This gives us a handle to the `ReactCSSTransitionGroup` object, which is what we will be using to animate changes in data, such as addition of cats, faving/unfaving, and so on."

"Let's start by animating the addition of new cats to the stream, shall we?"

```
render() {
    let Cats = this.state.catGenerator.Cats;

    return (
        <div>
            <div>
                <ReactCSSTransitionGroup transitionName="cats"
                                         transitionEnterTimeout={500}
                                         transitionLeaveTimeout={300}
                                         transitionAppear={true}
                                         transitionAppearTimeout={500}>
                {Cats.map(cat => (
                    <div key={cat.cid} style={{float: 'left'}}>
                        <Link to={`/pictures/${cat.cid}`}
                              state={{ modal: true, returnTo: this.props.
location.pathname, cat: cat }}>
                            <img style={{ margin: 10 }} src={cat.get('src')}
height="100"/>
                        </Link>
                        <span key={`${cat.cid}`} className="fa fa-star"></
span>
                    </div>
                ))}

</ReactCSSTransitionGroup>
            </div>
        </div>
    )
}
```

"Here, I changed our render method and simply wrapped the display of the collection of cats in a `ReactCSSTransitionGroup` element, like so."

```
<ReactCSSTransitionGroup transitionName="cats"
                         transitionEnterTimeout={500}
                         transitionLeaveTimeout={300}
                         transitionAppear={true}
                         transitionAppearTimeout={500}>
```

"Let's go through them one by one in the following:

- `transitionName`: This property is used to define the class name prefix used for the CSS classes applied for different events, such as element enter, leave, and so on.

- `transitionEnterTimeout`: This is the timeout for an element to be displayed freshly after rendering.

- `transitionLeaveTimeout`: This is similar to `transitionEnterTimeout`, but it is used when the element is removed from the page.

- `transitionAppear`: Sometimes, we want to animate the addition of the collection of elements, in our case cats, when they are first rendered. We can do this by setting this property to true.

Note that the elements, which are added after the first elements are displayed, are applied the `transitionEnter` property.

- `transitionAppearTimeout`: This is similar to the other timeout values, but for `transitionAppear`.

- `transitionEnter`: This is, by default, set to `true`. It can be set to `false` if we don't want to animate the element-enter transition.

- `transitionLeave`: This is, by default, set to `true`. It can be set to `false` if we don't want to animate the element-leave transition animation.

"Now, based on the transition and transition name, classes are applied to the elements within the `<ReactCSSTransitionGroup/>` component. For example, for enter transition, and our `cats` prefix, `cats-enter` would be applied to the elements."

"In the next cycle, `cats-enter-active` will be applied to the final class that the element should be in."

"Got it."

"Let's check all the different transitions that we can define based on this."

```
.cats-enter {
    opacity: 0.01;
}

.cats-enter.cats-enter-active {
    opacity: 1;
    transition: opacity 1500ms ease-in;
}
.cats-leave {
    opacity: 1;
}

.cats-leave.cats-leave-active {
    opacity: 0.01;
    transition: opacity 300ms ease-in;
}

.cats-appear {
    opacity: 0.01;
}

.cats-appear.cats-appear-active {
    opacity: 1;
    transition: opacity 1.5s ease-in;
}
```

"The animation transitions are pretty simple here. When a new element is added in the beginning, to start with the six cats that we initialized with, the .cats-appear class is applied. In the next tick, the .cats-appear-active class is added to the element."

"Next, the classes are removed after a successful transition, as shown in the following screenshot:"

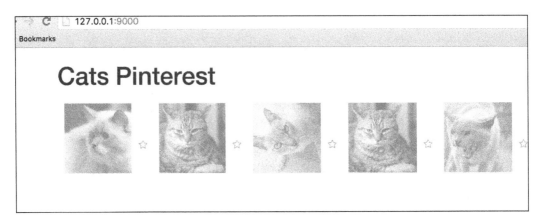

"Shawn, if you can see, you will notice how the cats fade in and then show up in their end state in full opacity."

"Cool. That looks nice. A nice effect for when the new elements are added, as well."

"True. Do you want to try animating the stars?"

"Sure!"

"Let me first check the classes that we have for the stars. I can see that you have made use of the font-beautiful star and added style to them."

```
.fa {
  transition: all .1s ease-in-out;
  color: #666;
}
.star{
    display: inline-block;
    width: 20px;
    position: relative;
}

.star span{
    position: absolute;
    left: 0;
    top: 0;
}

.fa-star{
```

```
    color: #fa0017;
}

.fa-star-o{
    color: #fa0017;
}

.fa-star-o:active:before {
    content: "\f005"!important;
}
```

"Yup, that's it right there."

"First, let me handle fave and unfave on the stars."

```
faveUnfave(event){
    let catCid = event.target.dataset;
    let catGenerator = this.state.catGenerator;
    let Cats = catGenerator.Cats;
    let cat = Cats.get(catCid);
    cat.set('faved', !cat.get('faved'));
    catGenerator.Cats = Cats;
    this.setState({catGenerator: catGenerator});
}
```

"Change the element to add `data-cid` and `handler`, as follows:"

```
<span key={`${cat.cid}`}  className="fa fa-star" onClick={::this.
faveUnfave} data-cid={cat.cid}></span>
```

"Firstly, I am passing `faveUnfave` as the `onClick` event, which is bound to the class context here. Next, I am passing `cat.cid` value for `data-cid`"

"In the `faveUnfave` method, I will then pull the cat ID for the faved element. Based on this, I will pull the cat object from the catGenerator's cat collection. Later, I will toggle the state of the current fave value and reset the state of the collection."

"This looks good."

"Next, I will display either the faved or unfaved star, based on the current fave status and wrap this as a CSS transition so that we can start showing animation to display and hide the star, change the color, and so on."

```
<ReactCSSTransitionGroup transitionName="faved"

transitionEnterTimeout={500}

transitionLeaveTimeout={300}
                                          transitionAppear={true}

transitionAppearTimeout={500}
                                          className="star">
                 {()=>{
                   if(cat.get('faved') === true){
                     return <span key={`${cat.cid}`}  className="fa
fa-star" onClick={::this.faveUnfave} data-cid={cat.cid}></span>;
                   } else {
                     return <span key={`${cat.cid}`}  className="fa
fa-star-o" onClick={::this.faveUnfave} data-cid={cat.cid}></span>;
                   }
                 }()}
                 </ReactCSSTransitionGroup>
```

"Perfect," followed Mike.

"Now let's add the styling for this fave."

```
.faved-enter {
    transform: scale(1.5);
}

.faved-enter.faved-enter-active {
    transform: scale(3);
    transition: all .5s ease-in-out;
}

.faved-leave {
    transform: translateX(-100%);
    transform: scale(0);
}

.faved-leave.faved-leave-active {
    transform: scale(0);
    transition: all .1s ease-in-out;
}
```

"Here, I added animation such that, on clicking the star, it will scale up, similar to Twitter's fave functionality. Then, it will scale back and remain in faved state."

"Similarly on unfave it will scale up and back to its original size."

"Looks good, let's check it out," followed Mike.

"Umm, I think all elements are here, but it doesn't seem to be working, Mike?"

"Let me see. Ah, so the culprit is this:"

```
{()=>{
    if(cat.get('faved') === true){
        return <span key={`${cat.cid}`} className="fa
fa-star" onClick={::this.faveUnfave} data-cid={cat.cid}></span>;
    } else {
        return <span key={`${cat.cid}`} className="fa
fa-star-o" onClick={::this.faveUnfave} data-cid={cat.cid}></span>;
    }
}()}
```

Notice the key value that we have used here? It's identical. The `TransitionGroup` keeps track of the changes to the elements and performs animation tasks based on key values. The `TransitionGroup` needs to know what has changed in the element in order to perform animation tasks and it also needs the key to identify the element.

"In the case here, the key will remain `cat.cid` in case of fave or unfave, and therefore the element stays the same."

"Let's add a suffix or prefix to the key, along with the fave status."

```
{()=>{
    if(cat.get('faved') === true){
        return <span key={`${cat.cid}_${cat.
get('faved')}`} className="fa fa-star" onClick={::this.faveUnfave}
data-cid={cat.cid}></span>;
    } else {
        return <span key={`${cat.cid}_${cat.
get('faved')}`} className="fa fa-star-o" onClick={::this.faveUnfave}
data-cid={cat.cid}></span>;
    }
}()}
```

"Perfect. It works now, Mike."

"Yup. Nice work on the CSS animation, Shawn. The star looks good. Let's see how it looks now."

"Here's how it looks when we fave a cat:"

"This one is after the fave transition is complete."

"Finally, the same animation takes place when we try to unfave the cat."

"Perfect, Carla will love this!"

It had been a fun day at Adequate LLC. Shawn and Mike worked on refactoring their app in order to allow data changes to reflect the view changes and animating the cats being added and removed. They also worked on how stars were faved/unfaved.

Summary

In this chapter, we worked around changing the data flow and passing data directly from react-router links. We took a look at animating a collection of objects being added/removed or as they appear. We saw different transition events supported by `ReactCSSTransitionGroup` and how to use relevant classes to animate our objects.

In the next chapter, we will learn how to test our app using Jest and React TestUtils.

11
React Tools

In the previous chapter, we learned how to use Animation add-on and CSS transition. We have also explored different events and studied how to easily enhance our application in order to create stunning effects using animations.

In this chapter, we will look at various tools in the React ecosystem, which are useful in the whole lifetime of an application—the development, debugging, and build tools. We will see how these tools make developing React applications a beautiful experience.

We will study the following tools in this chapter:

- Babel
- ESLint
- React Developer Tools
- Webpack
- Hot reloading using Webpack

Mike and Shawn had some free time before starting their next project. They decided to spend this time in learning more about various tools that they had used so far in their React projects for development, testing, and bundling the apps.

Development tools

"Shawn, today I would like to discuss about the tools that we have used until now while building our React apps today. React is a very small library, which does one thing right—rendering the UI. However, we had to use a lot of other tools with React throughout our journey until now. Today is the day to discuss everything about them." said Mike.

"Awesome, Mike! I am ready as always. Let's get rolling." exclaimed Shawn.

Using Babel for ES6 and JSX

"Shawn, we have used ES6 or ES2015 code since the beginning. We are also very bullish about using JSX. Sometimes, we have also used ES7 code, such as the function `bind` operator in our latest Cats Pinterest project."

```
// src/Home.js

class Home extends React.Component {
  componentDidMount() {
    this.timer = setInterval(::this.generateCats, 1000);
  }
}
```

"Yes, Mike. I loved the conciseness of these new features." said Shawn.

"However, current browsers still don't understand the ES6 or ES7 code that we have written. We use Babel to transform this code in ES5 JavaScript, which current browsers can run. It allows us to use the JavaScript syntax from the future today. Babel also has JSX support, therefore, it is very handy to use with React." explained Mike.

"Babel is very modular and comes with a plugin architecture. It has plugins for different ES6/ES7 syntaxes. Generally, we want to use React specific and ES6 specific plugins. Babel groups such common plugins into something called **presets**. Babel has various plugins for ES6, React, as well as different stages of future language proposals."

"We are mostly interested in using the ES2015 and React presets, which comprise of all the plugins related to ES6 and React. Occasionally, we do need some of the advanced features, such as the ES7 function bind syntax, so we need to configure it separately. In such cases, we use the individual plugins directly, as we used `transform-function-bind` for the function `bind` syntax."

 All of these presets and plugins come in their own npm packages. Babel is built this way — a small core and a giant plugin architecture with a lot of configuration options around it.

"Therefore, we will have to install all of these packages separately."

```
npm install babel-core --save
npm install babel-loader --save
npm install babel-preset-react --save
npm install babel-preset-es2015 --save
npm install babel-plugin-transform-function-bind -save
```

"Got it. I have also seen some Babel related configuration in our Webpack configuration." said Shawn.

"Yes. Though Babel allows us to convert files from the command line, we do not want to convert each and every file manually. Therefore, we have configured Webpack in such a way that it will convert our ES6/ES7 code using Babel before starting the app. It uses babel-loader package. Let's discuss it in detail when we discuss webpack later today," said Mike.

 We are using Babel version 6 throughout this book. Check out more details about Babel at `http://babeljs.io/`.

ESLint

"Shawn, you have seen my commits related to linting in our projects, right?"

"Yes. I used to get annoyed at these small little changes initially, but then I got used to them." said Mike.

"**Linting** is very important, especially if we want to maintain the code quality across different projects. Fortunately, linting React projects is very easy with ESLint. It also supports ES6 syntax and JSX so that we can also lint our next generation code." informed Mike.

"We are using eslint-plugin-react and babel-eslint npm packages to lint ES6 and React code. We have also globally installed the ESLint npm package."

 Check `http://eslint.org/docs/user-guide/getting-started` for details about getting started with ESLint.

"Mike, I also see that you have added lint command under scripts in `package.json`." added Shawn.

```
// package.json

"scripts": {
"lint": "eslint src"
}
```

"Yes, Shawn. It is common to miss a few things here and there in a big project. Having a command to lint the project helps us in finding such things. We need the eslint, eslint-babel, and eslint-plugin-react packages to use ESLint within our code. Therefore, we need to install it before trying to run this command."

```
npm install eslint --save
npm install babel-eslint --save
npm install eslint-plugin-react -save
```

"We are also using some standard configuration options for ESLint. These options are present in the .eslintrc file of our project. We define the rules that we want to check with ESLint in this file. We also enable ES6 feature that we want ESLint to whitelist. Otherwise, it will raise linting errors for such code as it natively only supports ES5. We also specify that ESLint should use babel-eslint as parser so that ES6 code will be parsed by ESLint properly."

```
// .eslintrc
{
  "parser": "babel-eslint",
  "env": {
    "browser": true,
    "es6": true,
    "node": true,
    "jquery": true
  },
  "plugins": [
    "react"
  ],
  "ecmaFeatures": {
    "arrowFunctions": true,
    "blockBindings": true,
    "classes": true,
    "defaultParams": true,
    "destructuring": true,
    "forOf": true,
    "generators": true,
    "modules": true,
    "spread": true,
    "templateStrings": true,
    "jsx": true
  },
  "rules": {
    "consistent-return": [0],
```

```
    "key-spacing": [0],
    "quotes": [0],
    "new-cap": [0],
    "no-multi-spaces": [0],
    "no-shadow": [0],
    "no-alert": [0],
    "no-unused-vars": [0],
    "no-underscore-dangle": [0],
    "no-use-before-define": [0, "nofunc"],
    "comma-dangle": [0],
    "space-after-keywords": [2],
    "space-before-blocks": [2],
    "camelcase": [0],
    "eqeqeq": [2]
  }
}
```

"We are all set now. Go ahead and run it on our Pinterest project and fix remaining linting issues." informed Mike.

```
$ npm run lint


> react-router-flux@0.0.1 lint /Users/prathamesh/Projects/sources/
reactjs-by-example/chapter11
> eslint src



/reactjs-by-example/chapter11/src/Home.js
  29:20  error  Missing space before opening brace  space-before-blocks


✖ 1 problem (1 error, 0 warnings)
```

"Ah, it complained about a missing space. Let me fix it quickly."

```
    // Before
    faveUnfave(event){
        ...
    }

    // After
    faveUnfave(event) {
        ...
    }
```

"Perfect, Shawn!"

 ESLint can also be integrated with your text editor. Check `http://eslint.org/docs/user-guide/integrations.html` for more details.

React Dev Tools

"Shawn, React is excellent at improving the developer experience. They have released react-dev-tools to help us in debugging our apps. React developer tools are Chrome and Firefox add-ons, which make debugging React apps fun."

"Once you install the add-on, you will then see a **React** tab in the browser console while running a React app. An interesting thing is that this tab is also shown for websites that use React in production too, for example, Facebook."

"Once we click on the **React** tab, it shows all the components in our app."

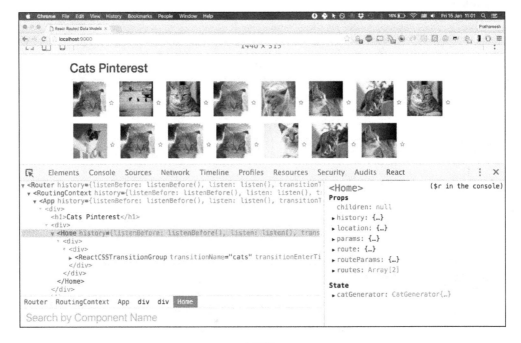

"Shawn, as you may have noticed, we can see all our components on the left-hand side pane. On the right-hand side, we see props and state of the component selected in the left pane. Therefore, we can inspect UI state at any point of time. We don't need to add `console.log` statements to see what is happening with our components."

"More than this, it provides us with a temporary variable — **$r**. The selected component from the console is available as **$r** in the console."

```
▼ <Router history={listenBefore: listenBefore(), listen: listen(), transition1    <App>                    ($r in the console)
  ▼ <RoutingContext history={listenBefore: listenBefore(), listen: listen(), t     Props
    ▼ <App history={listenBefore: listenBefore(), listen: listen(), transition1      ► children: {…}
      ▼ <div>                                                                         ► history: {…}
          <h1>Cats Pinterest</h1>                                                     ► location: {…}
        ▼ <div>                                                                       ► params: {…}
          ► <Home history={listenBefore: listenBefore(), listen: listen(), trans      ► route: {…}
          </div>                                                                      ► routeParams: {…}
        </div>                                                                        ► routes: Array[2]
      </App>
    </RoutingContext>
  </Router>
```

"Let's try to see what **$r** gives us in the console so that we can debug the selected component directly in console."

```
> $r
< ▼ Constructor {props: Object, context: Object, refs: Object, updater: Object, state: null…} 
    ► _reactInternalInstance: ReactCompositeComponentWrapper
    ► context: Object
    ► getDOMNode: function ()
    ► props: Object
    ► refs: Object
      state: null
    ► updater: Object
    ► __proto__: ReactClassComponent
```

"It also allows us to scroll to the selected component in the UI to see the actual source code of the component. It can also show all components of a specific type."

```
    ▼ <ReactCSSTransitionGroup transitionName="cats" transitionEnterTi   <ReactCSSTransitionGroupChild>
      ▼ <ReactTransitionGroup transitionName="cats" transitionEnterTime                   ($r in the console
        ▼ <span transitionName="cats" transitionEnterTimeout=500 transi   Props
          ► <ReactCSSTransitionGroupChild name="cats" appear=true enter=    appear: true
          ► <ReactCSSTransitionGroupChild name="cats" appear=true enter=    appearTimeout: 500
          ► <ReactCSSTransitionGroupChild name="cats" appear=true enter=  ► children: {…}
          ► <ReactCSSTransitionGroupChild name="cats" appear= enter=        enter: true
          ► <ReactCSSTra  Show all ReactCSSTransitionGroupChild     nter=   enterTimeout: 500
          ► <ReactCSSTra                                            nter=   leave: true
          ► <ReactCSSTra  Scroll to Node                            nter=   leaveTimeout: 300
          ► <ReactCSSTra                                            nter=   name: "cats"
  Router  RoutingContext  App  (  Show Source
  ReactCSSTransitionGroup  React  Show in Elements Pane
  ReactCSSTransitionGroupChild
  Search by Component Name
```

"So Shawn, what do you think about these dev tools?" asked Mike.

"I am very impressed. This is really nice! I will use them in each and every React project from now onwards." Shawn was very excited on seeing the power of React dev tools.

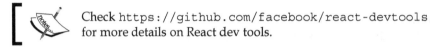

Check `https://github.com/facebook/react-devtools` for more details on React dev tools.

Build tools

"Shawn, the build system is arguably the first thing that we should care about when creating a new web application. It is not only a tool for running scripts, but in the JavaScript world, it usually shapes the basic structure of our application."

The following responsibilities should be performed by a build system:

- External dependencies as well internal dependencies should be managed
- It should run compilers/preprocessors
- It should optimize assets for production
- The development web server, browser reloader, and file watcher should be run by it

"There are a lot of different tools such as Grunt, Gulp, and Browserify, which can be used as part of our build system. Each tool has its own advantages and disadvantages. However, we have decided to go with Webpack in our projects." said Mike.

What is Webpack?

"Webpack is a module bundler. It bundles our JavaScript with its dependencies into a single package."

"Unlike Browserify and other tools, Webpack also bundles other assets such as CSS, fonts, and images. It supports CommonJS module syntax, which is very common in node.js and npm packages. Therefore, it makes things easier as we don't need to use another package managers for frontend assets. We can just use npm and share the dependencies between server-side code and front-end code. It is also smart enough to load dependencies in the correct order so that we don't need to worry about ordering explicit and implicit dependencies."

"As a result, Webpack alone can perform the task of Browserify as well as other build tools such as Grunt and Gulp."

This section will not cover every aspect of Webpack. However, we will discuss how to use Webpack effectively with React.

Webpack configuration

"Shawn, in a typical React app, we use ES6 code and JSX in our components. We also use frontend assets within the same component to make it more portable. Therefore, our Webpack configuration must handle the all these aspects correctly." explained Mike.

"Let's take an example of our Pinterest app and see how Webpack is configured to run it."

"First of all, we need to inform Webpack about the entry point of our app. In our case, it is the `index.js` file, which mounts the `App` component in the DOM."

```
// src/index.js
render((
  <Router history={history}>
    <Route path="/" component={App}>
      <IndexRoute component={Home}/>
      <Route path="/pictures/:id" component={Picture}/>
    </Route>
  </Router>
), document.getElementById('rootElement'));
```

"Therefore, we mention the entry point as `src/index.js` in the `webpack.config.js.` file."

```
// webpack.config.js
path = require('path');
var webpack = require('webpack');

module.exports = {
  // starting point of the application
  entry: [ './src/index']
};
```

"Secondly, we need to inform Webpack where to put the generated bundled code from our source. This is done by adding a config for output."

```
// webpack.config.js
var path = require('path');
```

```
var webpack = require('webpack');

module.exports = {
  entry: ['./src/index'],
  output: {
    path: path.join(__dirname, 'dist'),
    filename: 'bundle.js',
    publicPath: '/static/'
  }
}
```

"The output option tells Webpack to write the complied files in the current directory's dist folder. The name of the file will be bundle.js. We can see the output of bundle.js by running the webpack command."

```
$ webpack
Hash: f8496f13702a67943730
Version: webpack 1.12.11
Time: 2690ms
    Asset      Size   Chunks             Chunk Names
bundle.js  1.81 MB        0  [emitted]  main
   [0] multi main 52 bytes {0} [built]
    + 330 hidden modules
```

"This will create a dist/bundle.js file with all the compiled code."

"The publicPath specifies the public URL address of the output files, when referenced in a browser. This is the path that we use in our index.html file, which will be served by the web server to the users."

```
// index.html
<html>
  <head>
    <title>React Router/ Data Models</title>
    <link rel="stylesheet" href="https://maxcdn.bootstrapcdn.com/
bootstrap/3.3.5/css/bootstrap.min.css" type="text/css" />
    <link href="https://maxcdn.bootstrapcdn.com/font-awesome/4.5.0/
css/font-awesome.min.css" rel="stylesheet">
  </head>
  <body>
    <div id='rootElement' class="container"></div>
  </body>
  <script src="https://code.jquery.com/jquery-2.1.4.min.js"></script>
```

```
    <script src="https://maxcdn.bootstrapcdn.com/bootstrap/3.3.5/js/
bootstrap.min.js"></script>
    <script src="/static/bundle.js"></script>
    </html>
```

Loaders

"After this, we have to specify different loaders to transform our JSX, ES6 code, and other assets properly. Loaders are transformations that are applied to a resource file of your app. They are functions (running in node.js) that take the source of a resource file as the parameter and return the new source. We use `babel-loader` for our ES6 and JSX code."

```
// webpack.config.js
module.exports = {
  module: {
    loaders: [
      {
        test: /\.jsx?$/,
        loader: 'babel-loader',
        query: {
          presets: ['es2015', 'react'],
          plugins: ['transform-function-bind']
        },
        include: path.join(__dirname, 'src')
      }]
  }
};
```

"We have installed the `babel-loader` package via npm and included it in `package.json`. After this, we have specified it in our Webpack configuration. The test option matches the files with the given regex. The given loader parses these files. Therefore, `babel-loader` will compile `.jsx` and `.js` files from our source files in the `src` directory specified by the `include` option. We also specify that `babel-loader` should use es2015 and react presets as well as function-bind transformer plugin so that Babel will be able to parse all of our code properly."

"For other type of assets such as CSS, fonts, and images, we use their own loaders."

```
// webpack.config.js

module.exports = {
module: {
    loaders: [
```

```
    {
      test: /\.jsx?$/,
      loader: 'babel-loader',
      query: {
        presets: ['es2015', 'react'],
        plugins: ['transform-function-bind']
      },
      include: path.join(__dirname, 'src')
    },
    { test: /\.css$/, loader: "style-loader!css-loader" },
    { test: /\.woff(\d+)?$/, loader: 'url?prefix=font/&limit=5000&mi
metype=application/font-woff' },
    { test: /\.ttf$/, loader: 'file?prefix=font/' },
    { test: /\.eot$/, loader: 'file?prefix=font/' },
    { test: /\.svg$/, loader: 'file?prefix=font/' },
    { test: /\.woff(2)?(\?v=[0-9]\.[0-9]\.[0-9])?$/, loader: "url-
loader?limit=10000&minetype=application/font-woff"},
    { test: /\.(ttf|eot|svg)(\?v=[0-9]\.[0-9]\.[0-9])?$/, loader:
"file-loader" }
    ]
  }
};
```

"All of these loaders come in their own npm packages. We have to install npm packages for `style-loader`, `css-loader`, `url-loader`, and `file-loader` and update `package.json`."

 Check `https://webpack.github.io/docs/using-loaders.html` for more details about using and configuring loaders.

Hot module replacement

"Shawn, one of the coolest features of Webpack is **Hot Module Replacement (HMR)**. This means that whenever we modify a component and save the file, Webpack will replace the module on the page without reloading the browser and losing component state." informed Mike.

"Wow! That sounds very impressive." exclaimed Shawn.

"To get hot reloading working, we have to use the excellent react-hot-loader package and webpack-dev-server. The webpack-dev-server package saves us from running Webpack repeatedly for every file change before starting the server. It will run the app for us using the `config` options provided in `webpack.config.js`. The key point in setting up webpack-dev-server is configuring it for hot reloading. It can be done by adding a `hot: true config` option."

```
// server.js
var webpack = require('webpack');
var WebpackDevServer = require('webpack-dev-server');
var config = require('./webpack.config');

new WebpackDevServer(webpack(config), {
  publicPath: config.output.publicPath,
  hot: true,
  historyApiFallback: true
}).listen(9000, 'localhost', function (err, result) {
  if (err) {
    console.log(err);
  }

  console.log('Listening at localhost:9000');
});
```

"This will make sure that webpack-dev-server will start on localhost port `9000`, with hot reloading enabled. It will also use all the configuration that we defined in `webpack.config.js`." said Mike.

"We will have to modify our `package.json` to run the `server.js` script."

```
// package.json
"scripts": {
    "start": "node server.js",
  }
```

"This will make sure that the `npm start` command will run the `webpack-dev-server`.

"We also have to make some changes in our Webpack configuration in order to make hot reloading work. We have to configure the entry option to include dev server and hot reloading server."

```
entry: [
    'webpack-dev-server/client?http://localhost:9000',
    'webpack/hot/only-dev-server',
    './src/index'
]
```

"Next up, we need to inform Webpack to use hot-loader with other loaders that we have already added."

```
module: {
    loaders: [
        { test: /\.jsx?$/,
          loader: 'react-hot',
          include: path.join(__dirname, 'src')
        }
        .. .. ..
    ]
}
```

"Finally, the hot module replacement plugin from Webpack has to be included in the plugins section of the config."

```
plugins: [
    new webpack.HotModuleReplacementPlugin(),
    new webpack.NoErrorsPlugin()
]
```

"The final Webpack configuration looks like this"

```
// webpack.config.js
var path = require('path');
var webpack = require('webpack');

module.exports = {
  devtool: 'eval',
  entry: [
    'webpack-dev-server/client?http://localhost:9000',
    'webpack/hot/only-dev-server',
    './src/index'
  ],
  output: {
    path: path.join(__dirname, 'dist'),
    filename: 'bundle.js',
    publicPath: '/static/'
  },
  plugins: [
    new webpack.HotModuleReplacementPlugin(),
    new webpack.NoErrorsPlugin()
  ],
  resolve: {
    extensions: ['', '.js', '.jsx']
  },
```

```
module: {
  loaders: [
    { test: /\.jsx?$/,
      loader: 'react-hot',
      include: path.join(__dirname, 'src')
    },
    {

      test: /\.jsx?$/,
      loader: 'babel-loader',
      query: {
        presets: ['es2015', 'react'],
        plugins: ['transform-function-bind']
      },
      include: path.join(__dirname, 'src')
    },
    { test: /\.css$/, loader: "style-loader!css-loader" },
    { test: /\.woff(\d+)?$/, loader: 'url?prefix=font/&limit=5000&mi
metype=application/font-woff' },
    { test: /\.ttf$/, loader: 'file?prefix=font/' },
    { test: /\.eot$/, loader: 'file?prefix=font/' },
    { test: /\.svg$/, loader: 'file?prefix=font/' },
    { test: /\.woff(2)?(\?v=[0-9]\.[0-9]\.[0-9])?$/, loader: "url-
loader?limit=10000&minetype=application/font-woff"},
    { test: /\.(ttf|eot|svg)(\?v=[0-9]\.[0-9]\.[0-9])?$/, loader:
"file-loader" }
  ]
  }
};
```

"Now if we start the app using `npm start`, then it will use hot-reloader with webpack-dev-server. Shawn, try changing some code and check whether the code gets updated in the browser without refreshing the page. Magic!!" explained Mike.

"Great, Mike. Yeah, it really works. All hail Webpack and hot reloading!"

Summary

In this chapter, you learned about various tools from the React ecosystem—development, testing, and production tools that we have used in various stages of our app development. We discussed Babel, the JavaScript transpiler, to convert our next generation JavaScript code to ES5. We also saw how to use ESLint and React dev tools that make React development easy. In the end, we saw how Webpack can be used with React with its powerful loaders and configuration options. We saw how these tools can make developing React apps a beautiful experience.

In the next chapter, we are going to dive deep into Flux as an architecture. We have seen how problems arise during data sharing across components. We will see how to overcome them using Flux.

12
Flux

In the previous chapter, we took a look at the various tools in the React ecosystem that are useful in the whole lifetime of an application — development, testing, and production. We also saw how React improves the developer experience using developer tools. We learned about the various testing tools that can be used with React. To summarize it, we saw how to use build tools such as Webpack and Browserify and how they can be used with React.

In this chapter, we are going to dive deep in Flux as an architecture. We have seen how problems arise during data sharing across components. We will see how we can overcome them by having a single point of data store. Next, we will check out how to use React to overcome this.

Dispatcher acts as a central hub to manage this data flow and communication and how Actions invoke them. Finally, we will we take a look at the complete data flow that takes place, while building our Social Media Tracker application.

In this chapter, we will cover the following topics:

- Flux architecture
- Stores
- Actions
- Dispatcher
- Flux implementations

At the end of chapter, we will be able to start replacing parts of our application that have tight data coupling, with Flux We will be able to set up the necessary groundwork for Flux and easily start using the same in our React views.

Flux architecture and unidirectional flow

"Hey Mike and Shawn!" entered Carla, on a bright morning.

"Hi Carla, how are you today?"

"Wonderful. The previous app that you build was nice, the clients liked it. They will soon add more features to it. Meanwhile, we have got another small app to build."

"Oh, nice. What are we planning to build?" inquired Mike.

"We need to build a kind of social tracker. To start with, we show a user's reddits, tweets, and so on. We will later extend it to display other information."

"Got it," iterated Shawn.

"Have a good day; I will leave it to you."

"So Shawn, what do you think about the new project?"

"It should be exciting. Umm… can we explore Flux and use it in the app? We had discussed it when we were building the last app."

"Yeah, we can. This will be the perfect opportunity to see how Flux works. Before we start using it, let's go through what Flux actually is."

"Flux is a simple architecture for React to make use of unidirectional flow. We have discussed previously how unidirectional flow suits React. React follows the render-always model when there are any changes made to data. Data doesn't go other way around, like in the case of two-way bindings."

"It's not exactly the **Model-View-Controller** (**MVC**) way of working. It consists of Model (Stores), Actions and Dispatchers, and finally Views (React Views)."

"There is no module for complete Flux as a framework as it's not meant to be. Facebook provides the Flux module, which consists of the **Dispatcher**. Other parts such as **View** and **Stores** can be done without much support. Let's go over them one by one, shall we?"

"Sure. I believe we can go over how they correlate and why exactly are they useful when an app starts to grow."

"Yup."

"As you can see in the following image, the various components are tied together and function distinctly. Data flows in a single direction in a cycle."

"As I mentioned previously, a **Dispatcher** acts as the central hub. Whenever an event takes place from the View, such as a user clicks a button or an Ajax call is completed, an action from the Actions is called. The **Action** may also get called from the **Dispatcher**."

"The Actions are simple constructs that deliver the payload to the **Dispatcher**, which identify what the **Action** is and other details from the action and data needed to update current state."

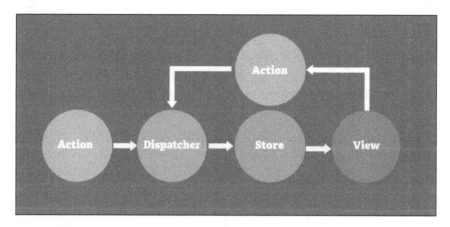

"The **Dispatcher** then propagates it to the stores. **Dispatcher** acts like a callback registry, where all stores register themselves. **Dispatcher** notifies and callbacks stores whenever some action takes place. Irrespective of the action, it is delivered to all the stores."

"The **Dispatcher** is not doing any complex activities, it just forwards the payload to registered stores, and it doesn't process any data."

"The responsibility to perform logical and complex decisions and data changes is entrusted with the stores. This helps to make the point of data changes at a single place and avoid changes all around the application, which are harder to track."

"On receiving a callback from the **Dispatcher**, the **Store** decides whether it needs to perform any action or not, based on the **Action** type. Based on the callback, it can update the current store. It can also wait for other stores to be updated. After it is done with the changes, it goes ahead and notifies the view. This can be achieved in our simple Flux version by making use of an EventEmitter module which is available from the events module."

"Similar to Actions, the Views register themselves to hear changes in stores. On some changes, an event is emitted by `EventEmitter`. Based on the event type, it will call a `View` method, which has registered to listen to an event."

"The **View** receiving the event can then update its own state, based on the current state of any stores that are available to it. The state update then triggers the **View** update."

"This process continues with a **View** event, resulting in calls to the **Actions** and **Dispatcher** and so forth."

"Hope, this is somewhat clear now?" queried Mike.

"Umm… yeah, let me wrap my head around it. We have actions to perform an **Action**, based on an event. It then notifies the **Dispatcher**, which then notifies any store registered to listen for the changes. The Stores then update themselves, based on the action type and notify the React Views to update themselves."

"Correct! Let's dive in the app right away. We will base our app from the official Flux example. It will be structured like this."

```
js/
├── actions
|   └── SocialActions.js
├── app.js
├── components
|   └── SocialTracker.react.js
├── constants
|   └── SocialConstants.js
├── dispatcher
|   └── AppDispatcher.js
├── stores
|   └── SocialStore.js
└── utils
    └── someutil.js
```

"Now, as Carla mentioned, we need to show the user's data from Twitter and Reddit. For Reddit, it's available openly via API calls, as we will see shortly."

"For Twitter, we are going to need to set up some groundwork and create a Twitter app. We can create a new one on `https://apps.twitter.com/`. I have already created one for our app."

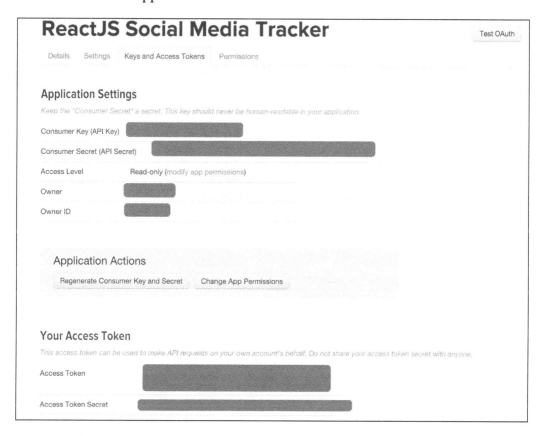

"We are then going to make use of the `twitter` module to access Twitter and fetch tweets from users. Let's set up a `config.js` file to store the preceding access tokens that we have created, as follows:"

```
module.exports ={
    twitter_consumer_key: 'xxxx',
    twitter_consumer_secret: 'xxxx',
    twitter_access_token_key: 'xxxx',
    twitter_access_token_secret: 'xxxx'
}
```

"These correspond to the relative keys and secrets that we created in our app. Next, we will create a client to access the data using the preceding credentials."

```
var Twitter = require('twitter');
var config = require('./config');

var client = new Twitter({
  consumer_key: config.twitter_consumer_key,
  consumer_secret: config.twitter_consumer_secret,
  access_token_key: config.twitter_access_token_key,
  access_token_secret: config.twitter_access_token_secret
});
```

"We are going to make use of this client in our express server application. As I said, for Reddit, we can hit Reddit API directly to access reddits. For Twitter, it will first hit our node App and return tweets to our React Components."

"Would you like to define this, Shawn?"

"Sure."

```
var express= require('express');
var app = new (require('express'))();
var port = 3000

app.get('/tweets.json', function (req, res) {
  var params = {screen_name: req.query.username};
  client.get('statuses/user_timeline', params, function (error,
tweets, response) {
    if (!error) {
      res.json(tweets);
    } else {
      res.json({error: error});
    }
  });
});
```

"I defined a JSON endpoint here called `tweets.json`. It will call the `client.get()` method, which is a REST API wrapper to call Twitter API. We invoke the `statuses/user_timeline` API to fetch the user timeline for a user, which is passed to us from the request.

On receiving the response, it will send this back to the React component calling it."

"Looks good. Now, let's start with the App. We will start by defining the Dispatcher."

```
// AppDispatcher.js
var Dispatcher = require('flux').Dispatcher;

module.exports = new Dispatcher();
```

"We define our dispatcher by requiring it from `flux.Dispatcher`. We will then use this at various places."

Flux actions

"Now we need to define the actions types that we are going to refer to as constants at various places, such as sending the type from Actions to store, and in our store, deciding what action type has been passed to store to take appropriate actions.

```
//SocialConstants.js
var keyMirror = require('keymirror');

module.exports = keyMirror({
    FILTER_BY_TWEETS: null,
    FILTER_BY_REDDITS: null,
    SYNC_TWEETS: null,
    SYNC_REDDITS: null

});
```

"Here, we are using the `https://github.com/STRML/keyMirror` package to create keys and values for the object based on the keys. This will convert into object similar to below."

```
{
FILTER_BY_TWEETS: 'FILTER_BY_TWEETS',
...
}
```

"This is handy when adding new keys to not repeat the same contents again."

"We can now start using the action constants. They represent four actions that we are going to perform, as follows:"

- SYNC_TWEETS: This fetches the tweets for a given user
- SYNC_REDDITS: This fetches the reddits for a give topic
- FILTER_BY_TWEETS: This only displays tweets, instead of tweets and reddits
- FILTER_BY_REDDITS: This only displays reddits, instead of tweets and reddits

"Next, let's define the actions that will be called from different places in our views."

```
// file: SocialActions.js
var AppDispatcher = require('../dispatcher/AppDispatcher');
var SocialConstants = require('../constants/SocialConstants');
var assign = require('object-assign');
var JSONUtil = require('../utils/jsonutil');

var SocialActions = {

  filterTweets: function (event) {
    AppDispatcher.dispatch({
      type: SocialConstants.FILTER_BY_TWEETS,
      showTweets: event.target.checked
    });
  },

  filterReddits: function (event) {
    AppDispatcher.dispatch({
      type: SocialConstants.FILTER_BY_REDDITS,
      showReddits: event.target.checked
    });
  },


  syncTweets: function (json) {
    AppDispatcher.dispatch({
      type: SocialConstants.SYNC_TWEETS,
      tweets: json.map((tweet) => {
        return assign(tweet, {type: 'tweet'})
      }),
      receivedAt: Date.now()
```

```
    });
  },

  syncReddits: function (json) {
    AppDispatcher.dispatch({
      type: SocialConstants.SYNC_REDDITS,
      reddits: json.data.children.map((child) => {
        return assign(child.data, {type: 'reddit'})
      }),
      receivedAt: Date.now()
    });
  },

  fetchTweets: function (username) {
    fetch(`/tweets.json?username=${username}`)
        .then(JSONUtil.parseJSON)
        .then(json => SocialActions.syncTweets(json)).catch(JSONUtil.
handleParseException)
  },

  fetchReddits: function (topic) {
    fetch(`https://www.reddit.com/r/${topic}.json`)
        .then(JSONUtil.parseJSON)
        .then(json => SocialActions.syncReddits(json)).catch(JSONUtil.
handleParseException)
  }
};

module.exports = SocialActions;
```

"Let's go through these actions, case-by-case:"

```
  fetchTweets: function (username) {
    fetch(`/tweets.json?username=${username}`)
        .then(JSONUtil.parseJSON)
        .then(json => SocialActions.syncTweets(json)).catch(JSONUtil.
handleParseException)
  }
```

"Here, we are using fetch, which is similar to Ajax that we have used before, to fetch tweets from our own `tweets.json` API, where we are passing the username for which we need to get the tweets. We are making use of JSON utility methods here that we have defined as follows:"

```
var JSONUtil = (function () {
  function parseJSON(response){
    return response.json()
  }
  function handleParseException(ex) {
    console.log('parsing failed', ex)
  }
  return {'parseJSON': parseJSON, 'handleParseException':
handleParseException}
}());

module.exports = JSONUtil;
```

"They help us convert responses to JSON, or in case of failures, logs them:"

After we receive a successful response from API, we call `SocialActions.syncTweets(json)` method, from the same module.

```
syncTweets: function (json) {
  AppDispatcher.dispatch({
    type: SocialConstants.SYNC_TWEETS,
    tweets: json.map((tweet) => {
      return assign(tweet, {type: 'tweet'})
    }),
    receivedAt: Date.now()
  });
}
```

"Next, `syncTweets` accepts the JSON. Then, it wraps the JSON into an object payload to be sent to dispatcher. In this object, we are creating a tweets array out of the payload. We are also tagging each object to depict its type as tweet so that we can mix and match the tweets and reddit in same arrays and identity which object it represents: a tweet or reddit."

```
assign(tweet, {type: 'tweet'})
```

"We use `Object.assign`, which merges two objects together. We use it from the `object-assign` package here."

"Now, we notify the Dispatcher about the payload to be ultimately delivered to the stores follows"

```
AppDispatcher.dispatch({ payload…});
```

"Similarly, we have the `syncReddits` method, as follows:"

```
fetchReddits: function (topic) {
  fetch(`https://www.reddit.com/r/${topic}.json`)
      .then(JSONUtil.parseJSON)
      .then(json => SocialActions.syncReddits(json)).catch(JSONUtil.
handleParseException)
  }
```

"This fetches the reddits from `https://www.reddit.com/r/${topic}.json`, for example `https://www.reddit.com/r/twitter.json`.

"After fetching, it delivers the data to `SocialActions.syncReddits(json))`, which creates the payloads for the dispatcher, as follows:"

```
syncReddits: function (json) {
  AppDispatcher.dispatch({
    type: SocialConstants.SYNC_REDDITS,
    reddits: json.data.children.map((child) => {
      return assign(child.data, {type: 'reddit'})
    }),
    receivedAt: Date.now()
  });
}
```

"Note, how we are passing the type attribute for the actions here. This is to notify the stores what action to take when they receive the payload."

"Got it. It would be interesting to see how we proceed on the basis of this object."

"Yup. Next, we have two simple methods that relay the events to the stores, as follows:"

```
filterTweets: function (event) {
  AppDispatcher.dispatch({
    type: SocialConstants.FILTER_BY_TWEETS,
    showTweets: event.target.checked
  });
},

filterReddits: function (event) {
  AppDispatcher.dispatch({
```

```
      type: SocialConstants.FILTER_BY_REDDITS,
      showReddits: event.target.checked
   });
},
```

"We are going to use these methods as `onClick` methods. On clicking the checkboxes, the value for the checkbox — either reddit or twitter — will be available in `event.target.checked`."

"We wrap these in a simple object, tag them with the type of action call, and send the same to the Dispatcher. This way, we will know if we are going to display the tweets, reddit, or none."

Flux stores

"Cool, it looks like now we are all set to create our store."

"Yup Shawn. We will start by defining the state object that we will keep on updating and using as a store."

```
var AppDispatcher = require('../dispatcher/AppDispatcher');
var EventEmitter = require('events').EventEmitter;
var SocialConstants = require('../constants/SocialConstants');
var assign = require('object-assign');
var _ = require('underscore');

var CHANGE_EVENT = 'change';

var _state = {
  tweets: [],
  reddits: [],
  feed: [],
  showTweets: true,
  showReddits: true
};
```

"We have also defined a `CHANGE_EVENT` constant that we use as an identifier to *listen* to events of the *change* type from the event emitter in our store."

"We then define a method to update the states, creating a new one."

```
function updateState(state) {
  _state = assign({}, _state, state);
}
```

"This merges the new properties that need to be updated and merged into the existing state and updated the current state."

"Cool, this looks somewhat similar to the `setState` React method," said Shawn.

"Yup. Now we are going to define our store that will update the current state."

```
var SocialStore = assign({}, EventEmitter.prototype, {

  getState: function () {
    return _state;
  },

  emitChange: function () {
    this.emit(CHANGE_EVENT);
  },

  addChangeListener: function (callback) {
    this.on(CHANGE_EVENT, callback);
  },

  removeChangeListener: function (callback) {
    this.removeListener(CHANGE_EVENT, callback);
  }
});
```

"Here, we are defining our `SocialStore` by inheriting from `EventEmitter`. This gives it the capability to be used by the components to register to listen on events, `CHANGE_EVENT` in our case. The `addChangeListener` and `removeChangeListener` methods take in methods that should be called on events and remove the listener, as follows:" `this.on(CHANGE_EVENT, callback);` and `this.removeListener(CHANGE_EVENT, callback);`

"Whenever we want to notify the listeners, we call."

```
this.emit(CHANGE_EVENT);
```

"Finally, our views can get the current state from the store using following function:"

```
getState: function () {
    return _state;
  }
```

"Finally, Shawn, let's tie this all together with our Single Dispatcher, as follows:"

```
AppDispatcher.register(function (action) {

  switch (action.type) {

    case SocialConstants.FILTER_BY_TWEETS:
      updateState({
        showTweets: action.showTweets,
        feed: mergeFeed(_state.tweets, _state.reddits, action.
showTweets, _state.showReddits)
      });
      SocialStore.emitChange();
      break;

    case SocialConstants.FILTER_BY_REDDITS:
      updateState({
        showReddits: action.showReddits,
        feed: mergeFeed(_state.tweets, _state.reddits, _state.
showTweets, action.showReddits)
      });
      SocialStore.emitChange();
      break;
    case SocialConstants.SYNC_TWEETS:
      updateState({
        tweets: action.tweets,
        feed: mergeFeed(action.tweets, _state.reddits, _state.
showTweets, _state.showReddits)
      });
      SocialStore.emitChange();
      break;

    case SocialConstants.SYNC_REDDITS:
      updateState({
        reddits: action.reddits,
        feed: mergeFeed(_state.tweets, action.reddits, _state.
showTweets, _state.showReddits)
      });
      SocialStore.emitChange();
      break;
    default:
    // no op
  }
});
```

"Whenever we have `AppDispatcher.dispatch` being called by the payload, the preceding method is invoked."

"Let's take a look at one of these actions."

```
case SocialConstants.SYNC_TWEETS:
  updateState({
    tweets: action.tweets,
    feed: mergeFeed(action.tweets, _state.reddits,
      _state.showTweets, _state.showReddits)
  });
  SocialStore.emitChange();
  break;
```

"What we are doing here is calling `updateState` to update the current state by providing it with the updated tweets and update the feed, based on the `mergeFeed` method."

"Let's take a look at it."

```
function mergeFeed(tweets, reddits, showTweets, showReddits) {
  let mergedFeed = [];
  mergedFeed = showTweets ? mergedFeed.concat(tweets) :
    mergedFeed;
  mergedFeed = showReddits ? mergedFeed.concat(reddits) :
    mergedFeed;

  mergedFeed = _.sortBy(mergedFeed, (feedItem) => {
    if (feedItem.type == 'tweet') {
      let date = new Date(feedItem.created_at);
      return date.getTime();
    } else if ((feedItem.type == 'reddit')) {
      return feedItem.created_utc * 1000;
    }
  })
  return mergedFeed;
};
```

"I have combined various operations here to be handled, based on whether `showTweets, showReddits` are selected."

"So, what this method does is that it accepts the tweets and reddit array data, as well as checks whether show reddits or show tweets is checked or not. We build the final feed based on these checked/unchecked fields into the `mergedFeed` array."

"Then, we sort this array of both mixed up tweets and reddits data—`mergedFeed`, using `underscorejs` method, `sortBy`, and we sort the array on the basis of time fields on the two types of objects. In case of tweets, this field is the `created_at` field, and in case of reddit, it's the `created_utc` field. We normalize the time in UTC timestamp for comparison."

"Coming back to the sync tweets action, after updating the state, we call the emitter method on store:"

```
SocialStore.emitChange();
```

"This calls our emitter from the store to eventually deliver updates to the components."

"Got it. I believe the next step is creating our Views."

"That's right. We will split our view into three components—`Header`, `MainSection`, and `SocialTracker` container component."

"We start with the `Header`, as follows:"

```
var React = require('react');
var ReactBootstrap =  require('react-bootstrap');
var Row =  ReactBootstrap.Row, Jumbotron =  ReactBootstrap.Jumbotron;

var Header = React.createClass({

  render: function () {
    return (
        <Row>
          <Jumbotron className="center-text">
            <h1>Social Media Tracker</h1>
          </Jumbotron>
        </Row>
    );
  }

});

module.exports = Header;
```

"It's a simple display component, containing the header."

"Ah, Mike. I notice you are using the react-bootstrap module. That looks neat. Instead of defining it in plain elements and bootstrap properties, it helps us to wrap them in the React Components with properties."

"Yup. We are using the `Jumbotron` and `Row` here. This Row will get wrapped in a bootstrap Grid component."

"Next, we are going to get our `MainSection` component set up, this will show the inputs to get the usernames for Twitter and Reddit topic, as well as check for them:"

```
var React = require('react');
...
var SocialActions = require('../actions/SocialActions');
var SocialStore = require('../stores/SocialStore');
var MainSection = React.createClass({

  getInitialState: function () {
    return assign({twitter: 'twitter', reddit: 'twitter'},
SocialStore.getState());
  },

  componentDidMount: function () {
    SocialStore.addChangeListener(this._onChange);
    this.syncFeed();
  },

  componentWillUnmount: function () {
    SocialStore.removeChangeListener(this._onChange);
  },

  render: function () {

    return (
        <Row>
          <Col xs={8} md={8} mdOffset={2}>
            <Table striped hover>
              <thead>
              <tr>
                <th width='200'>Feed Type</th>
                <th>Feed Source</th>
              </tr>
              </thead>
              <tbody>
              <tr>
                <td><Input id='test' type="checkbox" label="Twitter"
onChange={SocialActions.filterTweets}
                      checked={this.state.showTweets}/></td>
                <td><Input onChange={this.changeTwitterSource}
type="text" addonBefore="@" value={this.state.twitter}/>
```

```
                    </td>
                </tr>
                <tr>
                    <th><Input type="checkbox" label="Reddit"
onChange={SocialActions.filterReddits}
                        checked={this.state.showReddits}/></th>
                    <td><Input onChange={this.changeRedditSource}
type="text" addonBefore="@"
                        value={this.state.reddit}/></td>
                </tr>
                <tr>
                    <th></th>
                    <td><Button bsStyle="primary" bsSize="large"
onClick={this.syncFeed}>Sync Feed</Button>
                    </td>
                </tr>
                </tbody>
            </Table>
          </Col>
        </Row>
    );
  },

  changeTwitterSource: function (event) {
    this.setState({twitter: event.target.value});
  },

  changeRedditSource: function (event) {
    this.setState({reddit: event.target.value});
  },

  syncFeed: function () {
    SocialActions.fetchReddits(this.state.reddit);
    SocialActions.fetchTweets(this.state.twitter);
  },

  _onChange: function () {
    this.setState(SocialStore.getState());
  }

});

module.exports = MainSection;
```

"Now the component is doing a couple of things here. First, it's setting the state on the basis of the store."

```
getInitialState: function () {
   return assign({twitter: 'twitter', reddit: 'twitter'},
SocialStore.getState());
   },
```

"It is also tracking two different fields—Twitter and Reddit—username information. We bind these values based on inputs from the fields, as we have seen before:"

```
changeTwitterSource: function (event) {
   this.setState({twitter: event.target.value});
},

changeRedditSource: function (event) {
   this.setState({reddit: event.target.value});
},
```

"And then use this change handler on the input fields, like so."

```
<Input onChange={this.changeTwitterSource} type="text" addonBefore="@"
value={this.state.twitter}/>
```

"Next, we have our componentDidMount and componentWillUnmount functions register and de-register them to listen to the events emitted from the SocialStore:"

```
componentDidMount: function () {
   SocialStore.addChangeListener(this._onChange);
   this.syncFeed();
},

componentWillUnmount: function () {
   SocialStore.removeChangeListener(this._onChange);
},
```

"Here, we register the _onChange method to be called whenever the changes occur in the SocialStore. The _onChange method, in turn, updates the current state of the component, based on state of the store, as follows:"

```
this.setState(SocialStore.getState());
```

"Next, we specify the `SocialAction` methods to be called for events such as checking/unchecking Twitter/Reddit display and calling to sync the tweets and reddits. On calling out the syncing data, `syncFeed` gets called, which calls the related sync methods from `SocialActions`, passing in the current Twitter name and Reddit topic."

```
syncFeed: function () {
  SocialActions.fetchReddits(this.state.reddit);
  SocialActions.fetchTweets(this.state.twitter);
},
```

"Finally, we are going to wrap everything up with the `SocialTracker` component, as follows:"

```
var ArrayUtil = require('../utils/array');
var assign = require('object-assign');
var Header = require('./Header.react');
var MainSection = require('./MainSection.react');
var React = require('react');
var SocialStore = require('../stores/SocialStore');
var SocialActions = require('../actions/SocialActions');
var ReactBootstrap = require('react-bootstrap');
var Col = ReactBootstrap.Col, Grid = ReactBootstrap.Grid, Row =
ReactBootstrap.Row;

var SocialTracker = React.createClass({
  getInitialState: function() {
    return assign({}, SocialStore.getState());
  },
  componentDidMount: function() {
    SocialStore.addChangeListener(this._onChange);
  },
  componentWillUnmount: function() {
    SocialStore.removeChangeListener(this._onChange);
  },
  render: function() {
    return (
        <Grid className="grid">
          <Header/>
          <MainSection/>
          {this.renderFeed()}
        </Grid>
    )
```

```
  },

renderFeed: function() {
  var feed = this.state.feed;
  var feedCollection = ArrayUtil.in_groups_of(feed, 3);
  if (feed.length > 0) {
    return feedCollection.map((feedGroup, index) => {
      console.log(feedGroup);
      return <Row key={`${feedGroup[0].id}${index}`}>
        {feedGroup.map((feed) => {
          if (feed.type == 'tweet') {
            return <Col md={4} key={feed.id}><div className="well
twitter"><p>{feed.text}</p></div></Col>;
          } else {
            var display = feed.selftext == "" ? `${feed.title}:
${feed.url}` : feed.selftext;
            return <Col md={4} key={feed.id}><div className="well
reddit"><p>{display}</p></div></Col>;
          }
        })}
      </Row>
    });
  } else {
    return <div></div>
  }
},

_onChange: function() {
  this.setState(SocialStore.getState());
}

});

module.exports = SocialTracker;
```

"We have the same set up that we used previously to listen to the store updates and update the current state of the component."

"Nice, I see, all that's left is looping over the feed and displaying them," continued Shawn.

"I see that we are displaying the feed in groups of three in a row and applying individual styles, based on whether its a tweet and so on. To divide them in groups, we seem to be using ArrayUtil."

```
var ArrayUtil = (function () {
  function in_groups_of(arr, n) {
    var ret = [];
    var group = [];
    var len = arr.length;
    for (var i = 0; i < len; ++i) {
      group.push(arr[i]);
      if ((i + 1) % n == 0) {
        ret.push(group);
        group = [];
      }
    }
    if (group.length) ret.push(group);
    return ret;
  };

  return {'in_groups_of': in_groups_of}
}());

module.exports = ArrayUtil;
```

"Yup, that's right. With this, it looks like we are all set. We will finally display the component as usual."

```
var React = require('react');
var ReactDOM = require('react-dom');
var SocialTracker = require('./components/SocialTracker.react');

ReactDOM.render(
  <SocialTracker />,
  document.getElementById('container')
);
```

"Let's take a look at how it looks, shall we?"

"Here's how it looks, without tweets:"

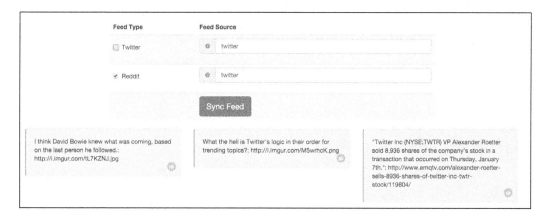

"Here's how it looks, when changing the twitter user:"

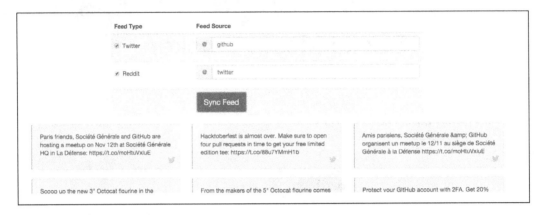

"This looks awesome, Mike!"

Summary

We did a deep dive in Flux as an architecture. We saw Dispatcher act as a central hub to transmit our data and Actions to process them. We saw how the main responsibility to manipulate the state and update itself was delegated to the stores themselves. Finally, we saw how they were tied up together and made it easy to be used in views and share stores across the components.

13
Redux and React

In the previous chapter, we dived into Flux as an architecture. We saw how problems arise during data sharing across components. We saw different parts of this architecture—Actions, Stores, Views, and Dispatcher—and build upon our example using pure Flux, Dispatcher from Facebook, and EventEmitter. Finally, we built a simple application to see how all these components are tied up together to create a simple flow to share a common state across components.

In this chapter, we will take a look at using Flux in a popular Flux-based state management implementation, **Redux**. We will see how it differs from pure Flux implementation that we saw previously. We will take a look at different components of Redux—its stores, actions, and reducers for the stores and actions. Finally, we will see how an app connects with the store, maintains a single state of the store, and passes information around in the views.

We will cover the following topics in this chapter:

- Redux
- Setting up Redux
- Redux store
- Reducers
- Connecting stores to app components
- Data flow in Redux

At the end of the chapter, we will be able to start using Redux in our applications to maintain the state for the Views. We will be able to set up and connect it with different parts of the app. We will be able to see how to distribute data in stores and use reducers and actions to manage the store's data.

Redux

"Good morning, Shawn," started Mike.

"Good morning, Mike. What are we working on today?"

"Ah, yesterday, we worked with Flux. It was to introduce you to the basics of Flux. In most of our projects, we used something similar to it in order to manage the state in the apps."

"Today, we will see how to use Redux."

"Cool."

"As stated at `https://github.coktreactjs/redux`, *Redux is a predictable state container for JavaScript apps.* It's kind of what we implemented previously."

"With Redux, we maintain a single state tree for the complete application and add reducers to enhance the state of the store. Previously, we were directly mutating the value of `_state` and then notifying the subscribers about the change. Let's take a look at our app setup to get started with, as follows:"

```
├── actions
│   └── social.js
├── components
│   └── SocialTracker.js
├── config.js
├── containers
│   └── App.js
├── reducers
│   ├── index.js
│   └── social.js
├── server.js
├── store
│   └── configureStore.js
├── styles
```

```
|     └── App.css
├── utils
```

This is based on our previous application and example from `https://github.acktreactjs/redux/tree/master/examples/todomvc.`"

"Umm, I don't see a dispatcher here."

"Correct. Redux deviates from the normal Flux; here, it does not have a dispatcher. During the set up, we will see how we connect stores to the components so that the components get updates for the changes to state in the store."

"Got it. Let's begin as before then?"

"Yup."

"Let's start with our Main Component; this will be wrapped to listen to store by Redux, as follows:"

```
        // App.js
import { bindActionCreators } from 'redux'
import { connect } from 'react-redux'
import SocialTracker from '../components/SocialTracker'
import * as SocialActions from '../actions/social'

function mapStateToProps(state) {
  return {
    social: state.social
  }
}

function mapDispatchToProps(dispatch) {
  return bindActionCreators(SocialActions, dispatch)
}

export default connect(mapStateToProps, mapDispatchToProps)
(SocialTracker)
```

Setting up Redux

"Now, there are different things happening here to set up our store. Let's go through them, one owing:.."

- `mapStateToProps`: We use this method to define how we are going to map the state from the Redux store to the props being sent to the components connected to listen to the store. Whenever new changes happen in the store, the components get notified and are passed to the object payload from this method.

- `mapDispatchToProps`: This method is used to map the Actions and pass them on the props so that they can be used from within the component.

- `bindActionCreators`: This is used to wrap our Actions creator (`SocialActions`) into dispatch calls to support calling the actions directly. This helps to call the actions and notify the store for updates, which are done due to the dispatch.

- `connect`: Finally, we have the connect call. This actually connects the React component to the store. It does not change the original component, but enhances and creates a new one. We can then start using the Actions from our component.

"Got it. So, we are creating two methods to map how the actions and state from Redux should be made available to the component. We are then connecting the store to Redux in order to listen to the updates and make the actions and stores available to the component when there are updates to the store."

"Yup. We are then going to start using this setup in the index, as shown in the following code:"

```
import React from 'react'
import { render } from 'react-dom'
import { Provider } from 'react-redux'
import App from './containers/App'
import configureStore from './store/configureStore'

const store = configureStore()

render(
  <Provider store={store}>
    <App />
  </Provider>,
  document.getElementById('root')
)
```

"The `Provider` component from the `react-redux` module allows us to connect the components to the stores. It accepts a store that we are setting up as the initial store state. The `Provider` component makes this store available to the components that are connected to hear from the store. This is what we did in our previous file by connecting to the store."

"Got it. This is where *Redux as a single store* comes into picture, I assume? I see that we have a single store that the complete app is going to make use of."

"Yup."

"Finally, we are going to complete our setup by defining the store that we are passing to the `<Provider>` tag, as follows:"

```
import { createStore, applyMiddleware } from 'redux'
import thunk from 'redux-thunk'
import reducer from '../reducers'

const createStoreWithMiddleware = applyMiddleware(
  thunk
)(createStore)

export default function configureStore(initialState) {
  const store = createStoreWithMiddleware(reducer, initialState)

  if (module.hot) {
    // Enable Webpack hot module replacement for reducers
    module.hot.accept('../reducers', () => {
      const nextReducer = require('../reducers')
      store.replaceReducer(nextReducer)
    })
  }

  return store
}
```

"Again, setting up a store requires performing different operations, let's go throulowing:."

* `createStore`: This creates a store for us to represent the complete state tree of the application. It takes in the arguments—the reducer (our reducers that we will see shortly) and initial state for the store.

- applyMiddleware: This is used to enhance Redux with middleware. Here, we are using the thunk middleware, which allows us to do asynchronous dispatches.

- configureStore: Finally, in configureStore, we are creating the store by calling the enhanced createStore: createStoreWithMiddleware. We have some conditions here to handle the hot module replacement to auto-reload the code changes, which we saw in HMR.

"Got it."

"Next, let's take a look at the following actions:"

```
import JSONUtil from '../utils/jsonutil'
import ArrayUtil from '../utils/array'

export const FILTER_BY_TWEETS = 'FILTER_BY_TWEETS';
export const FILTER_BY_REDDITS = 'FILTER_BY_REDDITS';
export const SYNC_TWEETS = 'SYNC_TWEETS';
export const SYNC_REDDITS = 'SYNC_REDDITS';

export function filterTweets(event) {
  return {
    type: FILTER_BY_TWEETS,
    showTweets: event.target.checked
  }
}

export function filterReddits(event) {
  return {
    type: FILTER_BY_REDDITS,
    showReddits: event.target.checked
  }
}


export function syncTweets(json) {
  return {
    type: SYNC_TWEETS,
    tweets: json.map((tweet) => {
      return {...tweet, type: 'tweet'}
    }),
    receivedAt: Date.now()
  }
```

```
    }

    export function syncReddits(json) {
      return {
        type: SYNC_REDDITS,
        reddits: json.data.children.map((child) => {
          return {...child.data, type: 'reddit'}
        }),
        receivedAt: Date.now()
      }
    }

    export function fetchTweets(username) {
      return dispatch => {
        fetch(`/tweets.json?username=${username}`)
            .then(JSONUtil.parseJSON)
            .then(json => dispatch(syncTweets(json))).catch(JSONUtil.
    handleParseException)
      }
    }

    export function fetchReddits(topic) {
      return dispatch => {
        fetch(`https://www.reddit.com/r/${topic}.json`)
            .then(JSONUtil.parseJSON)
            .then(json => dispatch(syncReddits(json))).catch(JSONUtil.
    handleParseException)
      }
    }
```

"We are importing the following code:"

```
    import JSONUtil from '../utils/jsonutil'
    import ArrayUtil from '../utils/array'
```

The JSONUtil and ArrayUtil class as before. I have moved them to use the classes instead of modules."

"The code for ArrayUtil class is as follows:"

```
    class ArrayUtil {
      static in_groups_of(arr, n) {
        var ret = [];
        var group = [];
        var len = arr.length;
        for (var i = 0; i < len; ++i) {
```

```
      group.push(arr[i]);
      if ((i + 1) % n == 0) {
        ret.push(group);
        group = [];
      }
    }
    if (group.length) ret.push(group);
    return ret;
  };
}


export {ArrayUtil as default};
```

"The code for JSONUtil class is as follows:"

```
class JSONUtil{
  static parseJSON(response){
    return response.json()
  }

  static handleParseException(ex) {
    console.log('parsing failed', ex)
  }
}


export { JSONUtil as default }
```

"Now, instead of the actions object that we defined before, we will define the actions as constants that we are going to refer across command:.."

```
export const FILTER_BY_TWEETS = 'FILTER_BY_TWEETS';

export const FILTER_BY_REDDITS = 'FILTER_BY_REDDITS';

export const SYNC_TWEETS = 'SYNC_TWEETS';

export const SYNC_REDDITS = 'SYNC_REDDITS';
```

"For other methods, we define the methods simply as follows:"

```
export function filterTweets(event) {
  return {
    type: FILTER_BY_TWEETS,
    showTweets: event.target.checked
  }
}
```

"Similar to our previous implementation, we wrap and return the payload that will be used by the reducer to mutate the store."

"In case of fetching data from the API, we wrap the actual calls in `dispatch`, as follows:"

```
export function fetchTweets(username) {
  return dispatch => {
    fetch(`/tweets.json?username=${username}`)
        .then(JSONUtil.parseJSON)
        .then(json => dispatch(syncTweets(json))).catch(JSONUtil.
handleParseException)
  }
}
```

"Here, we are dispatching the methods in an asynchronous manner and they will get chained and called when the results are returned. As we saw previously, when we call the following method from `SocialActions`, which we wrapped in the dispatch calls to notify the store:"

```
bindActionCreators(SocialActions, dispatch)
```

"In the preceding method, as it's not wrapped by default, we will wrap the methods inside `fetchTweets` in the `dispatch()` calls. We will also wrap the following code:"

```
dispatch(syncTweets(json))
```

"After a response is received, we will call syncTweets that also notifies the Redux store."

"Got it. Next, we should see the reducer, I guess?"

"Yup, let's take a look at it:"

```
import { FILTER_BY_TWEETS, FILTER_BY_REDDITS, SYNC_REDDITS, SYNC_
TWEETS } from '../actions/social'
import _ from 'underscore'

const mergeFeed = (tweets = [], reddits = [], showTweets = true,
showReddits = true) => {
  let mergedFeed = []
  mergedFeed = showTweets ? mergedFeed.concat(tweets) : mergedFeed;
  mergedFeed = showReddits ? mergedFeed.concat(reddits) : mergedFeed;

  mergedFeed = _.sortBy(mergedFeed, (feedItem) => {
    if (feedItem.type == 'tweet') {
      let date = new Date(feedItem.created_at);
      return date.getTime();
    } else if ((feedItem.type == 'reddit')) {
      return feedItem.created_utc * 1000;
    }
  })
```

```
      return mergedFeed;
};

export default function social(state = {
   tweets: [],
   reddits: [],
   feed: [],
   showTweets: true,
   showReddits: true
}, action) {
   switch (action.type) {
     case FILTER_BY_TWEETS:
       return {...state, showTweets: action.showTweets, feed:
mergeFeed(state.tweets, state.reddits, action.showTweets, state.
showReddits)};
     case FILTER_BY_REDDITS:
       return {...state, showReddits: action.showReddits, feed:
mergeFeed(state.tweets, state.reddits, state.showTweets, action.
showReddits)};
     case SYNC_TWEETS:
       return {...state, tweets: action.tweets, feed: mergeFeed(action.
tweets, state.reddits, state.showTweets, state.showReddits)};
     case SYNC_REDDITS:
       return {...state, reddits: action.reddits, feed:
mergeFeed(state.tweets, action.reddits,  state.showTweets, state.
showReddits)}
     default:
       return state
   }
}
```

"We already saw `mergeFeed` before. Similar to moving to classes, I moved the implementation to ES6. The logic for determining the feed is as before, we will accept Twitter and Reddit feeds and `showReddit`/`showTwitter` flags to determine how to construct the feed."

"Now, the peculiar method is as follows:"

```
export default function social(state = {
   tweets: [],
   reddits: [],
   feed: [],
   showTweets: true,
   showReddits: true
}, action)
```

"The reducer gets called for action dispatches. It receives the previous state in state and action payload in action. The state, as you can see here, has a default value."

"Now, based on the action payload, we will determine what needs to be run with the data, just as we did earlier:"

```
switch (action.type) {
    case FILTER_BY_TWEETS:
        return {...state, showTweets: action.showTweets, feed:
mergeFeed(state.tweets, state.reddits, action.showTweets, state.
showReddits)};
    ...
}
```

"The difference here is that we are not mutating the state directly. Based on the previous state, we merge the previous and current computed state, based on the action type and return it."

"This is now the current state of the app."

"Got it, I believe. All that we are left with is the app now."

"Yup, let's see how it will be. I have changed to use class as well."

```
class SocialTracker extends Component {
  constructor() {
    super();
    this.state = {twitter: 'twitter', reddit: 'twitter'}
  }
  componentDidMount() {
    this.syncFeed();
  }
  render() {
   let {filterTweets, filterReddits} = this.props;
    let {showTweets, showReddits} = this.props.social;
    return (
        <Grid className="grid">
          <Row>
            <Jumbotron className="center-text">
              <h1>Social Media Tracker</h1>
            </Jumbotron>
          </Row>
          <Row>
            <Col xs={8} md={8} mdOffset={2}>
              <Table striped  hover>
                <thead>
```

```
            <tr>
              <th width='200'>Feed Type</th>
              <th>Feed Source</th>
            </tr>
            </thead>
            <tbody>
            <tr>
              <td><Input id='test' type="checkbox" label="Twitter"
onChange={filterTweets} checked={showTweets}/></td>
              <td><Input onChange={::this.changeTwitterSource}
type="text" addonBefore="@" value={this.state.twitter}/></td>
            </tr>
            <tr>
              <th><Input type="checkbox" label="Reddit"
onChange={filterReddits} checked={showReddits}/></th>
              <td><Input onChange={::this.changeRedditSource}
type="text" addonBefore="@" value={this.state.twitter}/></td>
            </tr>
            <tr>
              <th></th>
              <td><Button bsStyle="primary" bsSize="large"
onClick={::this.syncFeed}>Sync Feed</Button>
              </td>
            </tr>
            </tbody>
          </Table>
        </Col>
      </Row>
      {this.renderFeed()}
    </Grid>
  )
}

changeTwitterSource(event) {
  this.setState({twitter: event.target.value});
}

changeRedditSource(event) {
  this.setState({reddit: event.target.value});
}

syncFeed() {
  const { fetchTweets, fetchReddits } = this.props;
  fetchReddits(this.state.reddit);
```

```
      fetchTweets(this.state.twitter);
      console.log('syncFeed was called');
  }


  renderFeed() {
    let {feed} = this.props.social;
    let feedCollection = ArrayUtil.in_groups_of(feed, 3);
    if (feed.length > 0) {
      return feedCollection.map((feedGroup, index) => {
        return <Row key={`${feedGroup[0].id}${index}`}>
          {feedGroup.map((feed) => {
            if (feed.type == 'tweet') {
              return <Col md={4} key={feed.id}><div className="well
twitter"><p>{feed.text}</p></div></Col>;
            } else {
              let display = feed.selftext == "" ? `${feed.title}:
${feed.url}` : feed.selftext;
              return <Col md={4} key={feed.id}><div className="well
reddit"><p>{display}</p></div></Col>;
            }

          })}
        </Row>
      });
    } else {
      return <div></div>
    }
  }


}

    export default SocialTracker
```

"So, we start by setting the local state to manage the Twitter user and Reddit us, as follows:."

```
constructor() {
    super();
    this.state = {twitter: 'twitter', reddit: 'twitter'}
  }
```

"In the `render` method, we fetch the values (the store) that are being passed down as props by Redux to the component in order to be displayed:"

```
let {filterTweets, filterReddits} = this.props;
let {showTweets, showReddits} = this.props.social;
```

"Now, if you recall the following:"

```
function mapStateToProps(state) {
  return {
    social: state.social
  }
}
```

"We are converting the state from Redux to pass the social object store from Redux as a prop to the component. We are then fetching the values such as showTweets, showReddits, and so on from the social prop value."

"Similarly, we have the following code:"

```
function mapDispatchToProps(dispatch) {
  return bindActionCreators(SocialActions, dispatch)
}
```

"This converts the actions and passes them down as the props. We are receiving them as `filterTweets` and `filterReddits` on props. We then make use of these actions as the `onclock` event handler, as follows:"

```
<Input id='test' type="checkbox" label="Twitter"
onChange={filterTweets} checked={showTweets}/>
```

"Finally, we have the display of the feed itself by fetching the values from the props in the same way:"

```
renderFeed() {
    let {feed} = this.props.social;
    let feedCollection = ArrayUtil.in_groups_of(feed, 3);
    if (feed.length > 0) {
      return feedCollection.map((feedGroup, index) => {
        console.log(feedGroup);
        return <Row key={`${feedGroup[0].id}${index}`}>
          {feedGroup.map((feed) => {
            if (feed.type == 'tweet') {
              return <Col md={4} key={feed.id}><div className="well
twitter"><p>{feed.text}</p></div></Col>;
            } else {
```

```
            let display = feed.selftext == "" ? `${feed.title}:
${feed.url}` : feed.selftext;
                return <Col md={4} key={feed.id}><div className="well
reddit"><p>{display}</p></div></Col>;
               }

           })}
         </Row>
       });
     } else {
       return <div></div>
     }
   }
```

"We will fetch the feed from the social prop being passed to us, as follows:"

```
    let {feed} = this.props.social;
```

"Finally, to sync the contents we have the following code:"

```
    syncFeed() {
      const { fetchTweets, fetchReddits } = this.props;
      fetchReddits(this.state.reddit);
      fetchTweets(this.state.twitter);
      console.log('syncFeed was called');
    }
```

"Awesome. I guess that with this, we are done!"

"Yup. Would you like to recap the setup?"

"Sure. We started by setting up how we want to map the actions and stores to the props being sent to the components. We then set up the store and connect it to the component."

"To set up the store, we made use of and applied the thunk middleware module to enhance Redux in order to allow us to dispatch the actions asynchronously."

"We then created actions to be called from the component and wrap the payloads and action type to be delivered to the store."

"We also created the reducers—social reducer—to actually manipulate, create, and return new Redux states."

"That's right! Let's take a look at how it looks, shall we?"

"Awesome! Carla is going to love this."

Summary

We took a look at using Redux and setting it up. We saw how it differs from pure Flux implementation that we saw previously. We took a look at different components of Redux—its stores, actions, and reducers for the stores and actions. Finally, we saw how the app connects with the store and we make use of actions and data provided to the component via props.

Index

A

action 221, 222
add-ons
  about 127, 128
  commands, available 132, 133
  immutability helpers 128-132
animate 193-201
app (application)
  building 10, 11
  setting up 65

B

Babel
  URL 112, 205
  used, for ES6 204, 205
  used, for JSX 204, 205
Backbone models
  and data models 182, 183
  creating 170, 171
  defined Backbone models,
        incorporating 172
Bootstrap modal
  adding 103, 104
build tools 210

C

cloneWithProps add-on 133
component life cycle
  about 54
  methods 55-62
components
  building 6-9
  controlled 68
  data, passing 15-20

  multiple components 25-30
  namespaced components 32-34
  uncontrolled 70
components, cloning
  about 134-139
  apps testing, helpers used 139
  Jest, setting up 139, 140
  React components, testing behavior 142
  React components, testing
        structure 141, 142

D

data
  passing, from react-router links 186, 187
  passing, to components 15-20
data models
  and Backbone models 182, 183
delivery details 85-90
development tools 203
dispatcher 221, 222
DOM component 105, 106
DOM operations
  performing 150, 151
  shouldComponentUpdate hook,
        using 157-161
  time taken to render, determining 151, 152
  wasted time, determining 152-157

E

ES6
  Babel, using for 204, 205
ES2015 35
ESLint
  about 205-207
  URL 205, 208

F

fat arrow syntax
  about 74
  URL 74
fetch 117
Flux
  actions 225-230
  architecture 220-224
  stores 230-242
  unidirectional flow 220-224
forms
  about 63-68
  events 74-76
  validating 79-81
  wizard 70-73

H

Hot Module Replacement (HMR) 214-217
HTML
  converting to JSX, URL 24
  tags, versus React components 24

I

immutability helpers 128-131
immutable data
  about 164-166
  reference link 166
immutable data structures
  URL 133
import
  URL 66
initial state
  setting 52

J

JavaScript
  expressions 31
  JSX, transforming into 23, 24
Jest
  automatic mocking feature, URL 141
  setting up 139, 140
  URL 140
JSX (JavaScript XML)
  about 22

Babel, using for 204, 205
  conditionals 40
  gotchas 38-40
  styles 36-38
  transforming, into JavaScript 23, 24

L

loaders
  about 213, 214
  URL 214
lorempixel service
  URL 170

M

mixins 91-102
model
  updates 187-192
Model-View-Controller (MVC) 220

N

non-DOM attributes 41, 42

O

Object.assign method
  URL 130
objects 35
Open Library API endpoint
  URL 4, 114

P

parent-child relationship 76-79
PERF add-on
  installing 148-150
props
  default props, specifying 49, 50
  interactive 68
  this.props.children, modifying 50, 51
  validation 47, 48
  versus states 53, 54
PureRenderMixin
  about 161
  anti-pattern 163, 164
  installing 161, 162
  reference link 164

R

React
about 2
add-ons 127, 128
apps performance, optimizing 147
data flow 46, 47
DOM operations, performing 150, 151
forms 63, 64
getting, to render on server 109-123
URL 6
React components
testing, behavior 142-144
testing, structure 142
versus HTML tags 24
React Developer Tools
about 208-210
URL 210
ReactJS 3, 5
React library 6
react-router
Pinterest example, URL 168
reddits
URL 229
Redux
about 244, 245
setting up 246-258
URL 244, 245
refs 105-107

S

self-closing tag 25
server
component, pre-rendering 124, 125
server-side rendering 124, 125
shallowCompare 163, 164

shallow rendering 144
shipping details 81-84
shouldComponentUpdate hook
using 157-161
Single Page Application (SPA) 1
spread attributes 35
spread operator
URL 35
starter project
URL 110
state
about 51
avoiding 52
initial state, setting 52
setting 52
versus props 53, 54
static data
displaying 12-15
store 221

T

this.props.children
modifying 50, 51

V

view 222
virtual DOM 148

W

Webpack
about 210, 211
configuring 211, 212
Hot module replacement (HMR) 214-217
loaders 213, 214